Library of
Davidson College

THE VICTORIAN MUSE

Selected Criticism and Parody of the Period

*A thirty-nine-volume facsimile set
essential to the study of one of the most
prolific periods in English literature*

*Edited by
William E. Fredeman, Ira Bruce Nadel, John F. Stasny*

A Garland Series

A History of the Stage During the Victorian Era

Joseph Knight

Garland Publishing, Inc.
New York & London
1986

For a complete list of the titles in this series
see the final pages of this volume.

This facsimile has been made from a copy in
the Northwestern University Library.

Library of Congress Cataloging-in-Publication Data

Knight, Joseph, 1829–1907.
A history of the stage during the Victorian era.
(The Victorian muse)
Reprint. Originally published as part of The stage
in the year 1900 / compiled by W. Eden Hooper.
London: Spottiswoode, 1901.
1. Theater—England—History—19th century.
I. Title.   II. Series.
PN2594.K65   1986   792'.0941   86-19466
ISBN 0-8240-8609-0 (alk. paper)

Design by Bonnie Goldsmith

The volumes in this series are printed on
acid-free, 250-year-life paper.

Printed in the United States of America

A

HISTORY OF THE STAGE

DURING THE VICTORIAN ERA

BY

JOSEPH KNIGHT, F.S.A.

AUTHOR OF "THE LIVES OF ACTORS" IN THE *DICTIONARY OF NATIONAL BIOGRAPHY*

ETC.

AUTHOR'S PREFACE.

THE account of the English stage during the Victorian era which follows is drawn principally from a personal observation, longer and more intimate than falls to the lot of many individuals. It is with English performances only that it is as a rule concerned, though such artists, American or French, as acted in English or with English associates, find occasional mention. The visits of the Comédie Française, and of the Saxe-Meiningen and other companies—the brilliant performances of artists such as Rachel, Ristori, Salvini, Rossi, Sarah Bernhardt, Miss Ada Rehan, Edwin Booth, Joseph Jefferson, Eleonora Duse, M. Coquelin, and others—are practically ignored. Little attention is paid to lyrical performances, comic opera, and burlesque. So far as regards essentially dramatic works no full record, no record indeed approaching completeness, is attempted. Hundreds of works now principally forgotten have perforce been passed over. The chief aim has been to note the dramatic renascence, which is a striking and gratifying feature of modern days, and to trace the managements, companies, actors, pieces, and performances, by which this has been carried out. If many plays of primary importance are omitted, and many actors deserving recognition fail to obtain it here, these shortcomings will aid in establishing my thesis by proving how rich must be the stage of to-day when such work can be passed over.

JOSEPH KNIGHT.

London, *December*, 1900.

THE LATE WILLIAM TERRISS.

Portrait by Alfred Ellis and Walery, London.
Assassinated December, 1897.

INDEX TO CHAPTERS.

CHAPTER I.
                                                                PAGES
MEMORIES OF THE MIDDLE YEARS OF THE
    NINETEENTH CENTURY ... ...   1—12

CHAPTER II.
THE RENASCENCE OF THE DRAMA: THE
    ROBERTSON AND BANCROFT EFFORTS ...   13—25

CHAPTER III.
THE GROWTH OF PLAY-HOUSES: 1865 ONWARDS   26—46

CHAPTER IV.
THE LYCEUM AND SIR HENRY IRVING ...   47—61

CHAPTERS V TO XI.
DRURY LANE, THE ADELPHI AND OTHER GREAT
    HOUSES UNDER SUCCESSIVE MANAGEMENTS   62—168

CHAPTER XII.
FINAL OBSERVATIONS ... ...   169—184

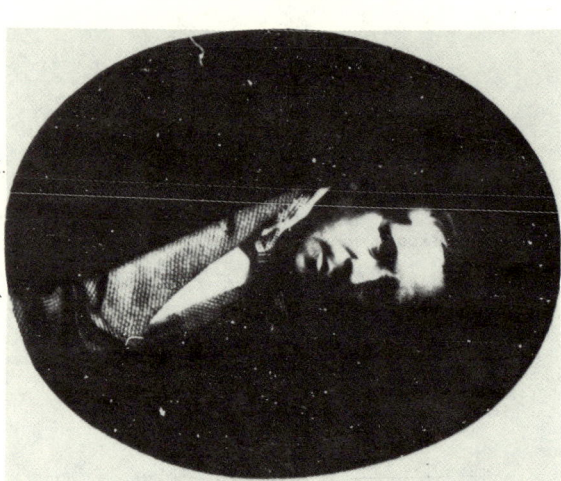

Jungmann Melátes

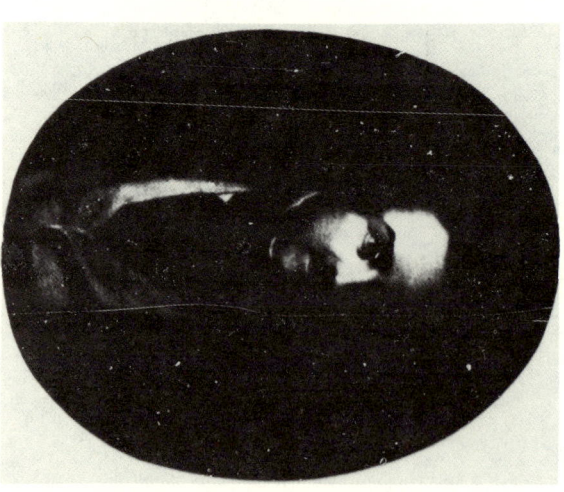

H. C. Havinesky

BENJAMIN WEBSTER.

Died 1882.

WILLIAM CHARLES MACREADY.

Died 1873.

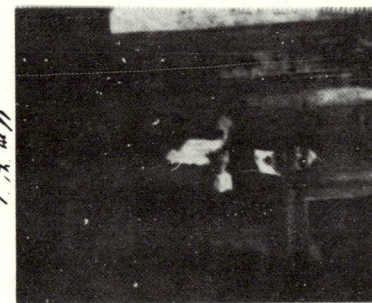

Mrs. Keeley

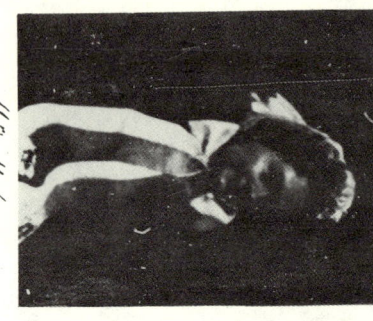

Mrs. Mellon

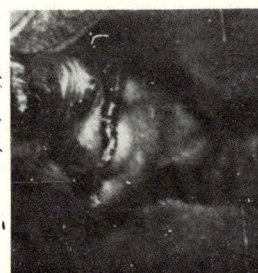

Miss Helen Faucit

Some late favourite players of the Shakespearean stage

Miss Lydia Thompson

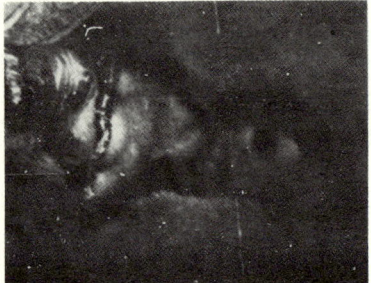

Mr. Keeley

MRS. KEELEY.

Died 1899.

ROBERT KEELEY.

Died 1869.

MISS HELEN FAUCIT (LADY MARTIN).

Died 1898.

MRS. STIRLING (LADY GREGORY).

Died 1895.

MISS LYDIA THOMPSON.

Long retired from active participation in her profession, but still happily spared to us.

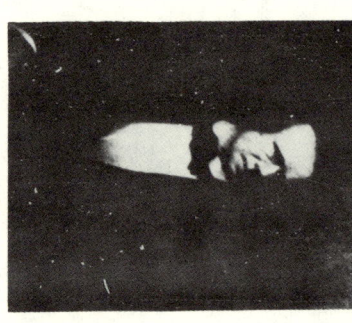

Samuel Mohr.

Bin-ka-ha-ne

Wihon

Some take prisoners they and the Indians town

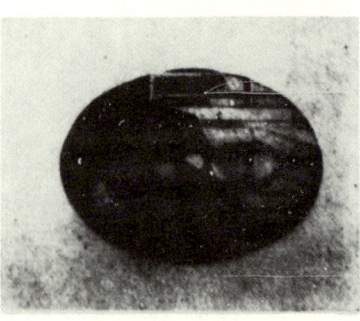

Chas Hallihan

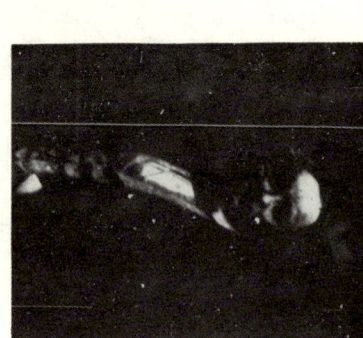

Chan Haan

SAMUEL PHELPS.

Died 1878.

CHARLES KEAN.

Died 1868.

FREDERICK THOMAS ROBSON.

Died 1864.

JOHN BALDWIN BUCKSTONE.

Died 1879.

CHARLES JAMES MATHEWS.

Died 1878.

THE STAGE IN THE YEAR 1900.

CHAPTER I.

It is a recognised fact that the periods of greatest literary interest in England have synchronised with the reigns of three female sovereigns, Elizabeth, Anne, and Victoria. In the reign of the sovereign last named, which, as it has been the longest in our annals, has been in many respects the most glorious, a strongly marked literary renascence has been accompanied by one no less distinct in art. The beginning of the latter is later in date and more strictly defined than that of the former. No courtiers are literature and art, to bend the servile knee and render in their birth homage to any monarch, however worthy or puissant. Putting the drama temporarily on one side, the growth of modern literature coincides accordingly with the life of Her Majesty rather than with her reign. At the period of her birth the literary firmament held a galaxy of stars such as in the conceits of Tudor times might well have been represented as assembled to greet the nativity of the greatest of queens. Byron, Scott, Wordsworth, Keats, Shelley, Coleridge, Southey, Campbell, and Moore, were among the poets—to deal with that class alone—of primary magnitude. Art, though we could then boast of a Turner, had declined from the days of Sir Joshua, Romney and Gainsborough, was on the point of a still further decay in its connection with the stage, and had to wait well on to half a century for its revival as regards domestic life. Not until the middle of the century did Britain enter upon the competition with other nations, as the result of which our existence has been brightened and our national wealth has been centupled.

With the overwhelming march of invention—though by this as by other things the stage has been benefited—there is no temptation or need to deal. The middle of the century marks the period when art lifted its head and began a slow but accelerating march. In the procession the drama and the stage subsequently took their place, with the result that the latter, long regarded as the Cinderella of the arts, is now installed as the fairy princess, and is the recipient of such homage as it has not known since it was an essential part of religious ceremonial.

Evidence is abundant of the divorce which half a century ago existed between the cultivated classes and the stage—a divorce none the less real and striking because it succeeded a period of conjugal association, affection and respect. At the present moment dramatic representations constitute the most prized of entertainments; the curiosity of the public concerning the lives of actors is insatiable; and the first presentation of a new play by a Pinero or a Jones, or a revival of Shakespeare by an Irving or a Tree, is a matter of universal and paramount interest. Diplomacy more subtle than is exercised in order to be present on a first night at the Haymarket, Wyndham's, or the St. James's was rarely employed in the last century to obtain admission to the most exclusive gathering at Almack's. Such change, moreover, as is indicated is not due to a display of caprice on the part of a public greedy of novelty and indefatigable in the pursuit of pleasure. The change of attitude is warranted. Half a century ago the spectacle might have been seen of a play shuffled on to the stage with no regard to propriety of character or costume by a company comprising doubtless some good actors, but with supernumeraries who stood on the stage and gaped at the pit or ogled the boxes, and who, when the most thrilling action was supposed to be passing under their eyes, paid no more heed to it than, to quote the words of Albery, "a monthly nurse pays to a single gentleman." The costume and general appearance of such became a byword, and the term an "Adelphi guest" was not, as is generally supposed, employed solely to characterise the "deadheads" in scarlet cloaks admitted to conceal the nakedness of the house, but was intended to depict the attendants at a mimic wedding, garden party, or coronation.

Such slackness or negligence was not everywhere visible. At the middle of the century Charles Kean was giving those revivals of *Henry VIII*, *Sardanapalus*, and *The Tempest*, which brought upon him the charge, subsequently transferred to other managers, of burying Shakespeare and Byron beneath upholstery. Representations creditable in every scenic respect had been given by Macready;

THE STAGE IN THE YEAR 1900: A SOUVENIR.

memories of the days when Charles James Mathews and Madame Vestris played in the brilliant extravaganzas of Planché were not distant; and *Acis and Galatea* at Drury Lane, with Clarkson Stanfield's scenery, had moved wonder and admiration. The comedies of Sheridan and Goldsmith were supported at the Haymarket by actors such as Farren, Buckstone, Chippendale and Compton. *Masks and Faces*, by Tom Taylor and Charles Reade, was given, with Webster as TRIPLET and Mrs. Stirling as PEG WOFFINGTON. Macready took his farewell as LEAR; Mr. Toole made his first appearance as SIMMONS in *The Spitalfields Weaver;* the Wallacks, from America, won recognition in Shakespearian and romantic drama; Miss Cushman arrived to play MEG MERRILIES and essay some unfeminine and unfamiliar experiments; Barry Sullivan attempted in *Hamlet* to substitute a London for an Irish and a Lancastrian reputation; Miss Lydia Thompson came forward for the first time in juvenile parts; and Miss Helen Faucit, subsequently Lady Martin, enriched the stage with a few exquisite creations, Shakespearian and other. The principal performers at the Adelphi included Wright, the foremost of low comedians, Mr. and Mrs. Alfred Wigan, Mrs. Keeley, Leigh

Murray, Miss Woolgar and Madame Celeste; Charles James Mathews, already beginning to look old, though always spoken of as preternaturally youthful; Sam Emery, the son of a distinguished father, and the father of a still more distinguished daughter; Phelps conducting at Sadler's Wells his memorable series of revivals; Robson raising burlesque into tragedy, as Fred Leslie a generation later raised it into comedy; and many other excellent actors were to be found at the Lyceum, the St. James's, the Olympic and the Strand. It would be a pleasant but unprofitable task to compare these actors with those of the period of Garrick, confessedly the brightest in our stage annals. Man for man and woman for woman, the actors of 1850 can scarcely be reckoned inferior to those of a century earlier. It would be futile, however, to assert that the later generation has left behind it memories such as cling to its predecessors. The secret of this seems to be found in the fact that literature at the latter epoch was practically divorced from the stage. Two lives of Garrick were written immediately upon his death, and an even larger number has been given by subsequent writers. Quin, Wilks, Barton Booth, Henderson, Foote, Mrs. Bellamy and Mrs. Baddeley found biographers, and Charles Lee Lewes left his memoirs. Interest even greater attended the actors of the period of Kemble and Kean. Mrs. Siddons found a Campbell to be her eulogist, and Kean a Barry Cornwall. James Boaden was indefatigable in writing biographies of the Kembles and others connected with the stage. Mrs. Jordan's life was more than once written, and John Bannister even has his memoir; while actresses such as Mrs. Billington and Miss Mellon (subsequently the wife of Coutts, the banker, and the Duchess of St. Albans) were the subjects of endless lampoons, libels and biographies, real or fictitious.

Sight must not, moreover, be lost of the fact that painters of high, and sometimes the highest, genius—Reynolds, Gainsborough, Hogarth, Romney, Zoffany, Clint and De Wilde—have preserved for us the features of the actors of the times mentioned, while critics extending from Steele and Churchill to Hazlitt, Leigh Hunt and Charles Lamb have dealt with their doings. At the middle of the nineteenth century literature and painting had ceased to concern themselves with the stage. Macready and Charles Mathews and his son, Charles James Mathews, left diaries which after their death, and in a period of renewed interest in the stage, were expanded into books. Charles Kean's career was depicted by John William Cole, an actor, in a work which is a sustained panegyric intended before all things to gratify its object ; and Young, Phelps, Munden and Compton ultimately became the subjects of biographies which were dictated rather by affection or piety than by any other cause.* Concerning the men, however, who were the props of the stage in 1850 nothing worth calling a record exists except such as is supplied in the *Dictionary of National Biography* or in newspapers which, as a rule, are unindexed and all but useless for purposes of reference. That the giants—for such they were—of a couple of generations ago have now fallen into oblivion which their predecessors more happily placed have escaped is due to the causes named, to the indifference of the public and the ineptitude of the critics. Of Benjamin Webster, the finest actor of his day— and his was a long day, his artistic career extending over more than half a century—no independent life has been written and no portrait doing justice to him is accessible. The same may be said of Buckstone, a ripe and exuberant comedian, the mere sound of whose voice would exhilarate an

* The life of Helen Faucit, by her husband, Sir Theodore Martin, has appeared while these pages are in the press.

audience before he came on the stage. Of Samuel Emery, who retained a great portion of the repertory of his father, the original TYKE in *The School of Reform*, what little is known is retained in the memory of admirers who are now veterans. Half a dozen portraits of John Emery in character, preserved in the Mathews Collection in the Garrick Club, and the criticisms of Leigh Hunt at least convey some idea of the personality and the qualifications of the elder. Biographies of a sort exist of Wright, Robson, and other actors of the time. They are, as a rule, catchpenny things, destitute of authority, and so scarce as to be practically inaccessible. The Wigans are forgotten like the snows of yester-year. The same holds true of most of those who were the delight of our fathers or grandfathers; and though in recent times something has been written about one or two it has been executed by those who are unable to speak at first hand, not having seen a solitary performance of the men whose biographers they elect to be.

For these reasons then the middle of the century may be regarded as the nadir of the modern English stage. It was the period in which public interest in it had sunk to the lowest state, and in which among cultivated Englishmen theatrical affairs were scarcely a subject of casual conversation or chance comment. Some few there were even in those days who might count as exceptions. These consisted for the most part of dramatists— Douglas Jerrold, Westland Marston (whose *Some Recollections of Our Recent Actors* is one of the best and most trustworthy books dealing incidentally with the period), Dickens, who was himself a fine actor, and George Henry Lewes, the grandson of a player who left some animated sketches of the principal actors of his day. Concerning the French stage of the time far more is known, and the records of Théophile Gautier, Jules Janin, and others, give full information as to a period of great dramatic activity which witnessed the production of the principal works of Musset, George Sand, Émile Augier, Octave Feuillet, Ponsard and Scribe. The stages of the two countries were at that time closely associated, since our own land had to depend almost exclusively upon adaptations from the French, the chief purveyors of which were Tom Taylor, Leicester Buckingham, John Oxenford, Stirling Coyne, Benjamin Webster, Bayle Bernard, Charles James Mathews, Charles Selby, Horace Wigan,

THE STAGE IN THE YEAR 1900: A SOUVENIR.

T. P. Wooler and John Maddison Morton. Altogether painful was the contrast between the two countries as regards the position of the drama and the influence of the stage. In France the chief writers of the day were, almost without exception, dramatists, and the most delicate and poetical intellect was content to pronounce judgment upon the works they produced. In England the leaders of thought held aloof from the stage. Scarcely a reference to it is to be found in the works of the great representatives of English literature; and even when a decade later the newspapers began to concern themselves with the question of its rehabilitation protests were not wanting against the prosecution of a task so gratuitous and so hopeless of accomplishment.

The sleep of the drama was long and all but unbroken. Such few works of merit as were seen between 1850 and 1865 gave no promise of an approaching dawn, and may be likened to the aurora borealis, which varies but scarcely relieves the monotony of the long Arctic night. Tennyson has told us how all

> The music of the moon
> Sleeps in the plain eggs of the nightingale:

and one has learnt that beneath the winter's snow prævernal influences prepare the way for the snowdrop and the daffodil. If any kindred influence underlay the drama, evidences of its existence are difficult to trace. The best days of Lord Lytton were over. Charles Reade, the one dramatist with invention, and Tom Taylor, the most daring and skilful of adaptors, gave the stage alone or in conjunction an occasional *Masks and Faces* or *Unequal Match*, and Westland Marston furnished *Donna Diana*, the source of which is found in Moreto, and a *Hero of Romance*, an adaptation from Octave Feuillet. Boucicault's most successful plays were adaptations of French pieces, such as *The Corsican Brothers*, and of Irish novels like *The Collegians*, which he turned into *The Colleen Bawn*. Scarcely one of the powerful or numerous dramas of Watts Phillips but was derived more or less directly from a French source, avowed or unavowed. Such coming lights as Thomas W. Robertson and W. S. Gilbert were as yet unrecognisable. Byron and Burnand were known as writers of burlesque, and the star of James Albery had not risen above the horizon.

THE STAGE IN THE YEAR 1900: A SOUVENIR.

CHAPTER II.

So slight were the symptoms of revival when they were first manifested that there is no cause for astonishment if their significance was not immediately recognised. The claims of the Robertsonian drama are still disputed. When it first dawned upon the world it was, half contemptuously, christened the "tea-cup and saucer school of comedy," and the name is not yet quite forgotten. Its merits, literary and dramatic, are not remarkable, and the work cannot be regarded as epoch-marking. When the future historian of the drama deals with this part of his subject he will have little to say concerning it. Yet the influence of the plays and the circumstances attending their production exercised a memorable and potent influence. That *Caste* and *School* paved the way for *The Second Mrs. Tanqueray*, *The Liars*, and *Sowing the Wind* cannot be said. They succeeded, however, in reconciling the world and the stage.

THE STAGE IN THE YEAR 1900: A SOUVENIR.

Prior to their time a first night's performance was a function to which men had to be dragged by some imperative call of duty or an active interest, possibly financial, in the stage. Before the short series was exhausted, literature, art and fashion had become reconciled with the drama, and the possession of a stall for an opening performance had become an object of diplomacy.

In this respect, then, the comedies of Robertson are of paramount interest, and the date of the pioneer of a dramatic renascence synchronises with the Bancroft management of the little Prince of Wales's theatre in Tottenham Street. Very far were the founders of that establishment from foreseeing the result of their labours. They "builded better than they knew." The new order sprang naturally and without effort out of the old. Miss Marie Wilton had for a few years been the mainstay of the Strand. She was idolised of the young Templars who flocked at nine o'clock, at half price, to see her marvellous performances in burlesque. As LUCY MORTON in *Court Favour* she established the fact that the saucy soubrette and the ineffable PRINCE PRETTYMAN was also a charming comedian. On the 15th April, 1865, this clever and fascinating creature opened the house—which had already been known by half a dozen different names, and was then called the Prince of Wales's—with a programme including a comedietta which introduced to the London public Mr. Bancroft, soon to become her husband, and a burlesque on the subject of *La Somnambula*. Her associates in her undertaking were Mr., now Sir, Squire Bancroft and H. J. Byron, who was the author of the burlesque, and who soon afterwards provided her with the comedy of *War to the Knife*. Naturally she surrounded herself with some of the sharers in her former triumphs. Her first company included John Clarke, F. Dewar, Miss Fanny Josephs, and Miss Bella Goodall; Mr. John Hare not joining her until the following year. No departure in art was involved in all this, and no scheme less revolutionary nor less likely to herald a change of any sort could have been devised.

It was not, indeed, until the production, on the 11th of December of the same year, of Robertson's comedy *Society* that the fortunes and the reputation of the management were established. The previous patrons of the house included those legal admirers of Miss Wilton who had flocked to her performances at the Strand and remained faithful to her during their progress to the highest offices of the law. It would be curious to trace how many of our judges and senators were present to witness the first performance of one or all of the series of Robertsonian comedies—*Society*, *Ours*, *Caste*, *Play*, *School*, and *M.P.* These pieces have been frequently revived, and, necessarily, with constantly changing casts. In the memory of the middle-aged playgoer no succeeding performances have eclipsed the original, and it is scarcely too much to say that the artists who took part in those early and delightful presentations formed in public estimation a sort of aristocracy of the stage. To have acted at the Prince of Wales's in a Robertsonian play under the Bancroft management was accepted as a certificate of merit and of honour.

One man, however prolific, could not provide for all the requirements of one of the most popular of London theatres. Between the Robertsonian comedies accordingly were sandwiched works of other writers. Among these may be noted Boucicault's *How She Loves Him*, first given on the 21st December, 1867, and *Tame Cats* by Edmund Yates, on the 12th December, 1868. No successor to Robertson revealing himself, the Bancrofts wisely did not attempt to promote an unworthy occupant to the vacant chair —or shall it be called throne? They fell back upon such works as existing dramatists could supply, or failing these upon revivals of Shakespeare, Sheridan, Bulwer Lytton, Reade and Taylor. *Man and Wife* by Wilkie Collins, produced 22nd February, 1873, with Mr. Coghlan as GEOFFREY, Mr. Bancroft as the DOCTOR, Mrs. Bancroft as BLANCHE LUNDIE, Miss Foote as ANNE SILVESTER, and Mr. Hare as SIR PATRICK LUNDIE, was the most noteworthy of the novelties. Mr. Gilbert's *Sweethearts*, a charming dramatic contrast, in which Mr. Coghlan was an admirable HARRY SPREADBROW and Mrs. Bancroft a delicious JENNY NORTHCOTT, supported on the 7th November, 1874, a revival of *Society*.

Wrinkles, by H. J. Byron, was given 13th April, 1876, and followed 30th September by *Peril*, a rendering by Messrs. Clement Scott and B. C. Stephenson of *Nos Intimes*, by M. Sardou. In this Mrs. Kendal was the heroine LADY ORMOND; Mr. Arthur Cecil presented an eccentric personage in SIR WOODBINE GRAFTON, a garrulous Indian civil servant; Mr. Sugden was CAPTAIN BRADFORD; Mr. Bancroft SIR GEORGE ORMOND; Mr. Kendal DR. THORNTON; Mr. Kemble and Mrs. Leigh Murray being the CROSSLEY BECKS, and Miss Buckstone LUCY ORMOND. This rendering of a difficult and an intractable piece caused some scandal, but was more than once revived. *The Vicarage*, a pleasing adaptation of *Le Village* of Octave Feuillet, showed on the 31st March, 1877, Mr. Arthur Cecil and Mrs. Bancroft to highest advantage as a cosy couple disturbed by the arrival of a travelled bachelor friend, happily played by Mr. Kendal.

Presented 12th January, 1878, *Diplomacy*, an adaptation of M. Sardou's *Dora*, kept the fortunes of the house at their highest. With an excellent cast —including Mrs. Bancroft as COUNTESS ZICKA, Mrs. Kendal as DORA, Mr. Bancroft as ORLOFF, Mr. Kendal as CAPTAIN BEAUCLERC, Mr. Clayton as the ELDER BEAUCLERC, Mr. Cecil as BARON STEIN, and Mr. Sugden as ALGIE—it obtained a popularity equal to that of almost any Robertsonian piece. It, too, has been frequently revived, the scene now known as that of "the three men" creating a profound sensation.

Albery's *Duty*, an adaptation of Sardou's *Le Bourgeois de Pont-Arcy*, introduced on the 27th September, 1879, many new actors—Mrs. Vezin, Miss Marion Terry, Mrs. John Wood, Miss Linda Dietz, Mr. Forbes-Robertson and Mr. Conway—but was not a success. A translation of *Anne-Mie* by Mr. Clement Scott, and *A New Trial* by Mr. Coghlan, did not concern the original management. The same may be said of *The Colonel* (*Le Mari à la Campagne* of Bayard) by Mr. Burnand, which in the hands of Miss Amy Roselle, Miss Myra Holme, Mr. Coghlan and Mr. Fernandez, enjoyed a remarkable popularity.

Revivals of well-known masterpieces had meanwhile been no less successful than novelties. *The School for Scandal*—with Mrs. Bancroft as LADY TEAZLE, Mr. Hare as SIR PETER, Miss Josephs as LADY SNEERWELL, Mrs. Leigh Murray as MRS. CANDOUR, Mr. Bancroft as JOSEPH, Mr. Coghlan as CHARLES, Mr. Collette as SIR OLIVER, and Mr. A. Wood as CRABTREE—was one of the earliest and the most discussed. That *The Merchant of Venice* was a failure was due to the shortcomings of Mr. Coghlan as SHYLOCK. Miss Ellen Terry's PORTIA was dreamlike in beauty and imagination. Mr. Bancroft was the PRINCE OF MOROCCO, and Miss Carlotta Addison NERISSA. For this piece was substituted *Money* (a second revival), in which Mrs. Bancroft was LADY FRANKLIN, in place of GEORGINA; Miss Ellen Terry CLARA DOUGLAS; Miss Carlotta Addison GEORGINA

Vesey; Mr. Coghlan ALFRED EVELYN; Mr. Collette SIR JOHN (previously played by Mr. Hare); Mr. Honey GRAVES; Mr. Bancroft SIR FREDERICK BLOUNT; and Mr. Archer DUDLEY SMOOTH. Mrs. Bancroft's PEG WOFFINGTON, in *Masks and Faces*, was another distinguished success. Miss Terry was MABEL VANE; Mr. Coghlan SIR CHARLES POMANDER; and Mr. Bancroft TRIPLET.

In *London Assurance* Mrs. Bancroft was PERT; Mrs. Kendal LADY GAY SPANKER; Mr. Kendal CHARLES; Mr. Bancroft DAZZLE; Mr. Cecil SIR HARCOURT COURTLEY; Mr. Honey MARK MEDDLE; Mr. Kemble DOLLY SPANKER; and Mr. Sugden COOL.

The management of the Haymarket, the first comedy theatre of London, succeeded on the 31st of January, 1880, that of the little bandbox of a house in which the reputation of the Bancrofts had been made, and was no less conspicuously capable and successful.

Chance, it has been seen, had something to do with the new theatrical development, since, had the Bancroft management not encountered and encouraged the Robertsonian muse, the movement towards a higher drama and stage would have been retarded, if not prevented. That the management in question

THE STAGE IN THE YEAR 1900: A SOUVENIR.

would under any circumstances have exercised a beneficial influence is not to be doubted. Care in the selection of pieces and actors, taste and liberality in the decorations, and an intelligent and orderly stage management, would always have been supplied. The soft and musical voice, inspiring laugh, and marvellous sense of humour of Mrs. Bancroft, who had enriched the world with a dozen exquisite and unsurpassable creations, of which ROSIE FANQUHERE, CECILIA DUNSCOMBE, NAOMI TIGHE, MAUD HETHERINGTON, and POLLY ECCLES are the best remembered, would have done honour to any stage in Christendom; and Mr. Bancroft, in many presentations of "swells," notably in CAPTAIN HAWTREY, had supplied a type as original, in its way, and as popular as LORD DUNDREARY. The result that the public would no longer stand the manner in which a piece had been, so to speak, pitchforked on to the stage, and that the continued presence of Bœotian supernumeraries staring with bovine stupidity directly away from the action which they were supposed to witness and in which they were presumed to participate became impossible, would necessarily have attended their efforts. But the sudden revival of interest on the part of the educated public might well have been deferred had the management had to depend on the Yateses, Collinses, and Byrons, to whom previously it had turned.

Besides rendering inconceivable the continuance of a state of affairs such as previously existed, the direction of the Prince of Wales's started and disciplined managers of taste and conditions kindred with its own and inspired in others a spirit of generous rivalry. Mr. Hare, whose subsequent career was to contend in brilliancy and *éclat* with that of the Bancrofts, was nursed in their bosom; the triune management of H. J. Montague, David James and Thomas Thorne, too soon dissolved, was directly influenced by imitation. Mr. Kendal got from them a portion of the training that has made him so admirable a comedian, and Mrs. Kendal—though she was a perfectly competent actress when she appeared at the Prince of Wales's—had an opportunity, by which she profited, of acquiring some of the traditions of management.

Actors who obtained a portion, at least, of their early training under the Bancroft influence included Mr. Forbes-Robertson, Blakeley, Mr. Coghlan, Mr. Collette, Mr. Standing, Mr. Kyrle Bellew, Arthur Cecil, Mr. Charles Sugden, Mr. H. Kemble, George

THE STAGE IN THE YEAR 1900: A SOUVENIR.

Honey, John Clayton, Mr. H. B. Conway, Mr. Brookfield, Arthur Dacre, Mr. Pinero, Mr. Teesdale, Mr. Elliot, Mr. Stewart Dawson, Mrs. Leigh Murray, Mrs. Langtry, Mrs. Bernard Beere, Mrs. Stirling, Miss Ellen Terry, Miss Carlotta Addison, Miss Henrietta Hodson, Miss Lydia Foote, Miss Litton, Miss Kate Phillips, Miss Marion Terry, and Miss Calhoun. Most of these lived to turn to account the lessons they had learned.

From the comparatively humble and tentative commencement at the Prince of Wales's to the superb performances and picturesque exhibitions that have since at various times been seen at the Lyceum, Her Majesty's, the Haymarket, the St. James's, the Criterion, Wyndham's and the Court theatres is a simple matter of theatrical progression. So soon as it was felt that the public sought for and appreciated " a good show " managements were found to supply it. Of good acting there has never in our stage history been a dearth. The value of *ensemble* was slowly grasped, the visits of foreign artists—French, German and Dutch—assisting us to realise its importance. It was longer before renewed interest in the stage produced a great or in any sense a national drama. In respect to the drama, however, improvement became visible. Under the fostering care of Sir Henry Irving, Wills gave us a *Faust*, a *Charles I* and a *Eugene Aram*; his *Olivia* was independent of such influences. Mr. Gilbert supplied a large variety of poetical and fantastical pieces and invented an entirely new form of comic opera which, in combination with the music of the late Sir Arthur Sullivan, obtained great popularity. He also presented serious comedies, to which society awarded more grudging recognition, but which are deserving of more consideration than has been bestowed upon them; while writers such as James Albery, Mr. Herman Merivale, Mr. F. C. Burnand, Mr. Bronson Howard, Charles Godfrey, Mr. Hamilton Aïdé, Mr. Robert Buchanan, Henry Pettitt and Mr. Dubourg, filled up the time until the younger generation of dramatists arose, to which our stage still looks for its supply. Some of these have provoked considerable discussion and incurred censure—ecclesiastical, senatorial and judicial. If, however, England during the nineteenth century can claim the possession of a drama which may stand erect by that of other nations it is due to our latest school of dramatists, all of whom happily are still among us and in active and remunerative employment.

THE STAGE IN THE YEAR 1900: A SOUVENIR.

The year 1865 accordingly, a period practically a generation ago, may be regarded as that of the birth of the stage of to-day. At that period the meteoric career of Fechter, who exercised a powerful influence, principally for good, and who brushed relentlessly away the cobwebs of irreverent tradition, was all but over, and that of Sir Henry Irving, whose influence was to be still more potent, can scarcely be held to have begun. We stand at the division of the ways. Of those by whom the highest form of drama was upheld, one half were near the period of enforced or voluntary retirement; a second half, all eagerness and hope, were pressing forward to fill their places, and among these, to deal with actresses alone, were those to whom the stage of to-day has owed most. Miss Helen Faucit (Lady Martin), though she came forth from her retirement to play JULIET, ROSALIND and IMOGEN, had all but severed her connection with the footlights. A couple of seasons later Miss Kate Terry—who had enriched the stage with many beautiful presentations of the heroines of romantic drama (BLANCHE DE NEVERS in *The Duke's Motto*, LADY PENARVON in *The Hidden Hand*, MARGARET WENTWORTH in *Henry Dunbar*, MARY LEIGH in *Hunted Down*, KATE

VERNON in *A Sister's Penance*, by Taylor and Dubourg, and DORA in an adaptation of Tennyson's poem so named), and had also won golden opinions as OPHELIA and JULIET, and doubled the parts of SEBASTIAN and VIOLA in *Twelfth Night*—withdrew into private life, her place being filled by her sister Ellen, destined to become the most renowned of a family every member of which has contributed to the delight of the playgoer, and the mention of which is more closely connected than perhaps any other with the advance that the closing years of the century have witnessed. Another actress belonging to the year in question, whose fame is happily still at its zenith, is Miss Madge Robertson (Mrs. Kendal), who made her professional *début* in London as OPHELIA to the *Hamlet* of Walter Montgomery. Miss Lilian Adelaide Neilson had triumphed at the Royalty as JULIET, but her short and brilliant career was only at the outset; while another conspicuous favourite of the public in a different line—Miss Nellie Farren —had at the Olympic given promise of the gifts which a few years later were to secure for her overpowering demonstrations of appreciation and affection. Ada Cavendish, afterwards the wife of Frank Marshall, was on the stage, but as yet had only

THE STAGE IN THE YEAR 1800: A SOUVENIR.

been seen in burlesque, and notably as Venus in Mr. Burnand's *Ixion*, a performance which, when she was in later years accepted in Shakespeare and romantic drama, she was not too eager to recall. When to the list already given, it is added that a period of twelve months witnessed the introduction to the London public of artists such as Mrs. John Wood, Mr. Charles Wyndham and David James, ample justification seems supplied for the selection of what must necessarily and under all circumstances be an arbitrary date.

To finish with and dismiss this part of the subject, it may be said that Miss Herbert, then at the St. James's, was at the height of her reputation, playing parts in high comedy such as Beatrice, Lady Teazle, Miss Hardcastle, Lydia Languish and Letitia Hardy; that Miss Bateman, though she had not yet established her reputation as Leah, stood high in public favour; that Joseph Jefferson in 1865 broke on the London public with his marvellous presentation of Rip Van Winkle; that Mrs. Stirling, beginning to find out she was no longer acceptable as a youthful heroine, remained unrivalled in Peg Woffington and other middle-aged parts; that Phelps at Drury Lane was surrounded by a crowd of so-called tragic actors, from the ruck of which surges up the name of Mrs. Hermann Vezin. Her husband, Mr. Hermann Vezin, was, it is believed, at no time a member of Phelps's Drury Lane company, though he played with that actor at Sadler's Wells, as well as with Charles Kean at the Princess's, and was the LAERTES to Fechter's HAMLET.

These things lead too far afield, since, however interesting as a survival of the so-called palmy days of the Kembles and Keans, Shakespearian presentations, as they were at this time understood, were in no wise conducive to the welfare of the stage, and such influence as they exercised was antagonistic to the movement it is sought to trace.

CHAPTER III.

INFLUENCES of the new example that had been set at the Prince of Wales's are not easily traceable during the years immediately following. New plays, many of them with claims on attention, were produced at the various London houses, the list of which slowly augmented. Byron, whose most prolific time this was, was the chief source of supply, two, and on one occasion three, of his pleasant, facile, brightly-written plays, brimming with absurdity, drollery and verbal quibble, the tinsel of which served almost better than gold, having been produced within a few days of each other. Quite impossible was it to quarrel with productions which kept the audience simmering with laughter and overflowing with delight. As a contribution to the drama of yesterday they were of little account, and as a preparation for that of to-day they were less than nought. Boucicault continued to supply plays, chiefly Irish in subject, one of which,

Arrah na Pogue, ranks in its line as a masterpiece, was translated into French, and was given successfully in Paris. Pieces of a more ambitious class were supplied by Westland Marston, Watts Phillips, Charles Reade, Tom Taylor, Mr. A. W. Dubourg, Mr. H. T. Craven, and other writers.

At the time when the transformation of the Prince of Wales's theatre took place, the West End houses, properly so called, in addition to this, were Drury Lane, Covent Garden, Her Majesty's, the Haymarket, the Lyceum, or English Opera House, the Adelphi, the St. James's, the Olympic, the Strand, and the Royalty. Nothing will give a better idea of the stagnation which existed in things theatrical than the fact that for close on a quarter of a century not a solitary addition had been made to the list. Some of those enumerated had had a hard struggle for existence, and not a few of them were frequently unlet.

The Strand—originally the scene of Burford's panorama, and subsequently known as Rayner's New Subscription Theatre, Punch's Playhouse, and by other names—was the object of so much persecution that manager after manager retired ruined. Strange devices were employed to combat the refusal by the Lord Chamberlain of a licence. As money could not be taken at the doors it was taken *at a window*. At times the sale for four shillings at an adjoining confectioner's of an ounce of rose lozenges gave the purchaser the right of entry, and seats bought for the Victoria theatre were sometimes available for the Strand.

The opening of the Prince of Wales's had not added a new theatre to London; it had only converted into a fashionable resort a house that had had as manifold and painful experiences as the Strand. No long time was, however, allowed to elapse before the success of the Bancroft management led to other experiments. Within a few years half a dozen new theatres were opened, and though many of them have since disappeared, and others are on the point of disappearance, some permanent additions were made to West End houses of theatrical entertainment. Nothing indeed more conclusively establishes the accuracy of the date fixed for the renascence of the theatre than the rage for building new houses which at once manifested itself. First in the field was the Holborn, which, under the management of Mr. Sefton Parry, opened on the 6th October, 1866, with Boucicault's drama, *The*

Flying Scud, a great and, as the event proved, a unique success. Vainly was the house renamed the Mirror and the Duke's; vainly did Miss Fanny Josephs, one of the most pleasing and graceful of actresses, undertake the management; vainly did Mr. Barry Sullivan, with the aid of Mrs. Hermann Vezin, try the legitimate drama, and vainly did Mr. Horace Wigan produce his adaptations from the French. The house perished unregrettedly by fire, and its site is now swallowed up in the First Avenue Hotel.

A more serious experiment was made the following year, 1867, when on the 24th of October the Queen's Theatre, erected on the site of St. Martin's Hall, Long Acre, was opened under the nominal management of Mr. Alfred Wigan. That the real manager was Mr. Henry Labouchere was a *secret de Polichinelle*. *The Double Marriage* of Charles Reade, the opening piece, was written on conventional lines. A comedietta, *He's a Lunatic*, was so far a concession to the new spirit that was in the air that it was the work of an untried author, Felix Dale, a pseudonym of Mr. Herman Merivale, who has since given the stage many imaginative and poetical works. With old stagers such as Wigan, who was in the first company, were also mixed younger actors, by some of whom the coming reform was to be carried out—Miss Ellen Terry, John Clayton, Mr. Charles Wyndham and Mr. Lionel Brough, who made on that occasion his *début* in London. *The Turn of the Tide*, one of the most conspicuous of Mr. Burnand's triumphs, added to the company Miss Henrietta Hodson, as well as such established actors as Ryder, Hermann Vezin, and Mr. and Mrs. Frank Matthews. A notable event in the brief records of the house was the appearance, in 1869, of "the beautiful" Mrs. Rousby as FIORDELISA in *The Fool's Revenge*. She subsequently played QUEEN ELIZABETH in Taylor's *'Twixt Axe and Crown*, and JOAN OF ARC in another piece by the same author.

Many worthy experiments were made at this house, at which Mr. Toole and Mr. Lionel Brough long divided the "comic lead," where Phelps played BOTTOM, and Miss Henrietta Hodson was NYDIA, in *The Last Days of Pompeii*, VIRGINIA and IMOGEN, where Mrs. John Wood first, and subsequently Miss Ellen Terry, played PHILLIPPA CHESTER in Charles Reade's *Wandering Heir*, and where Sir Henry Irving definitely established his reputation in London. Most interesting event of all is it that here Sir

Henry Irving and Miss Ellen Terry first played together, a memorable occasion, being the presentation by them, respectively, of PETRUCHIO and KATHARINE in Garrick's rascally adaptation of *The Taming of the Shrew*. Before it finally closed its doors in 1878 the Queen's had contributed some notable achievement to the restoration of the drama.

It was otherwise with the Globe, which was the next house to be built. On the 28th of November, 1868, it opened with H. J. Montague as the hero of *Cyril's Success*, a piece which, though it may perhaps rank as Byron's masterpiece, is built on purely conventional lines. Many vicissitudes has the theatre known. It was here that Miss Jenny Lee gave her harrowing presentation of Jo, that Miss Geneviève Ward triumphed in *Forget-me-Not*, that Tennyson's *Promise of May* failed greatly to please, and that *Charley's Aunt* did most of its running. Here finally *The Gay Lord Quex* established Mr. Pinero as one of the foremost of living dramatists. If its outset was not too promising the Globe has at least, before it is swept away in the resistless tide of London progress, risen to the times and associated itself with the most advanced mission of the English drama.

THE STAGE IN THE YEAR 1900: A SOUVENIR.

Theatres at this time were springing up like mushrooms, though few of them seemed as yet influenced by the new movement. Less than a month later than the Globe—on the 21st December, 1868—the Gaiety theatre, erected on the site of the Strand music hall, opened under the management of Mr. John Hollingshead. Sanguine hopes had been built upon an experiment which for the first time during many years entrusted to a literary man the direction of a theatre. At the outset these seemed in no way of being realised. The opening programme might indeed be branded with triviality. In the company, however, we have names shortly to become famous—Madge Robertson, Ellen Farren, Marie Litton and Constance Loseby. No long time elapsed before Mr. Hollingshead—who engaged Phelps, Charles James Mathews, W. Farren, and all the principal actors of the old school—was able to boast that he was paying his leading men salaries ranging from that of a Prime Minister to that of a Lord Chancellor. He produced very capably a series of Restoration comedies fitted to the modern stage, and kept always alight "the lamp of burlesque," which has ever burnt brightest at this theatre. In a performance of *Uncle Dick's Darling*, taken to some extent by H. J. Byron from Dickens's *Doctor Marigold*, he introduced a marvellous cast, comprising Miss Neilson as MARY BELTON, Mr. Toole as DICK DOLLAND, Mr. Henry Irving as MR. CHENEVIX, John Clayton as JOE LENNARD, and Miss Litton as ALICE RENSHAW. A finer interpretation has rarely been accorded a piece of this description. Shakespearian performances were given from time to time; and in a representation of *The Merry Wives of Windsor* Mr. Phelps as FALSTAFF, Mrs. John Wood as MRS. PAGE, Miss Rose Leclercq as MRS. FORD, Mr. Vezin as FORD, Mr. Forbes-Robertson as FENTON, and Miss Furtado (Mrs. John Clarke) as "Sweet" ANNE PAGE, linger pleasantly among recollections already beginning to seem remote. In subsequent days burlesque, amplified and enlarged so as to constitute an entire evening's entertainment, attained the utmost popularity it has known. Longer memories than are ordinarily bestowed upon playgoers seem to have been exhibited in the case of poor Fred Leslie and his constant and faithful associate, Nellie Farren; and the death of the former, followed as it was by the disappearance of the other, eclipsed the gaiety, if not of nations, at least of London. Not to be forgotten is the demonstration when, after her illness and bereavement, Miss Farren reappeared before her patrons. If ever there was an actor who gave burlesque the right to rank as art it was Fred Leslie, while Miss Farren had inimitable sauciness, spirit and go.

The Opéra Comique, which opened in October, 1871, and has now disappeared, is best remembered in connection with music, having established its reputation upon the early pieces due to the Gilbert and Sullivan combination. It is also dear to the amateur of fine acting on account of some early performances in Shakespearian comedy of Mrs. Kendal. It witnessed a few pieces of purely dramatic interest by Mr. Burnand, Mr. Joseph Hatton, and other writers; saw Mrs. Bernard Beere's artistically repellent performance in *As in a Looking Glass*, by Mr. F. C. Phillips; was the scene of production of *The Strike at Arlingford*, by Mr. George Moore, and *The Black Cat* of Dr. Todhunter; and saw further performances by the "independent theatre" and other irregularly constituted bodies.

Already gone is the Charing Cross theatre, which, under that name, enjoyed but little popularity. Renamed the Folly, it was the home of Miss Lydia Thompson, and was afterwards occupied by and named after Mr. Toole, who stayed in it for many years, and exhibited there several of his most successful impersonations. With a company of old favourites Mr. Toole produced Mr. J. M. Barrie's inimitable *Walker, London*, and other pieces, and the house retained this much-loved actor's name until its absorption into the adjacent hospital.

A further addition to the list of London theatres had been made on the 16th of April, 1870, when the Vaudeville opened, under the management of Messrs. H. J. Montague, David James and Thomas Thorne. This association of three young, earnest and ambitious actors seemed to promise a more formidable rivalry to the Prince of Wales's theatre than had yet been attempted. The opening performance was, however, injudicious and inept. *For Love or Money*, a poor comedy by Andrew Halliday, the least inspired among recognised and acted dramatists, was the main item in the earliest programme. A complete revenge for defeat was taken in the following June, when Albery's *Two Roses* was set before the public. Of all pieces written under the inspiration of Robertson this was the best and the most like the original. No performance, moreover, of the then young school of actors, except such as had been seen at the Prince of Wales's, had equal merit, whether as regards *ensemble* or the significance of individual impersonations. Mr. Montague and Mr. Thorne as the two lovers, Miss Amy Fawsitt and Miss Newton (afterwards Mrs. Thorne) as their sweethearts, won general acceptance. Mr. Henry Irving gave a superb presentation of DIGBY GRANT, a character in which during later years he has again been seen, and Mr. George Honey, in the absence of Mr. David James, was humorous as "Our" MR. JENKINS. This piece held out the promise, more than once suggested, that in Albery we had got a second Robertson. The following year Montague seceded from the management of the Vaudeville and went to the Globe. During many years Messrs. James and Thorne enjoyed exceptional good fortune. *Our Boys*, in which both actors appeared, ran longer than any piece had at that time run. No worse fortune attended the revival of the old comedies in which Mr. William Farren and Mrs. Stirling took parts. *Sophia*, adapted by Mr. Robert Buchanan from Fielding's *Tom Jones*, is entitled to be classed with the masterpieces of the century. The PARTRIDGE of Mr. Tom Thorne was the best performance that actor has given, the SOPHIA of Miss Kate Rorke was delightful, and the TOM JONES of Mr. Charles Warner eminently successful. During his connection with the Vaudeville Mr. David James supplied many performances unsurpassable in unction. JOHN TWEEDIE in Albery's *Tweedie's Rights*, GOLDFINCH in *The Road to Ruin*, PERKYN MIDDLEWICK and THEODORE MACCLESFIELD, count among the ripest presentations our stage has seen. During recent years the house has been devoted to farcical comedy, and has enjoyed with Mr. Weedon Grossmith much success.

After some flickering the theatre, afterwards named the Court, began to give a steady light. Miss Marie Litton there exploited the fertile invention of Mr. W. S. Gilbert. Her first experiment consisted in the production of *Randall's Thumb*, a comedy written in a more serious vein than such pieces, of the same author as *The Princess*, previously given at the Olympic, and *The Palace of Truth*, which belonged to the Haymarket. *Creatures of Impulse*, a musical fairy tale in Mr. Gilbert's more familiar line, followed, and was itself succeeded by *On Guard*, another serious and not too successful piece, in which Mr. Clayton, Mr. Alfred Bishop, Mr. Righton, Miss M. Oliver and Miss Kate Bishop were seen to advantage. Quitting for a while the Court—to which Westland Marston and Wills gave *Broken Spells* — Mr. Gilbert contributed *Pygmalion and Galatea* and *The Wicked World* to the Haymarket and one or two burlesques to the Gaiety, returning under a pseudonym of Tomline to the Court with *The Happy Land* and *The Wedding March*. The former, written in conjunction with Mr. Arthur à Beckett, and produced on the 3rd March, 1873, is the nearest approach to Aristophanesque satire that has been seen on our stage. Its humorous treatment of three well-known statesmen made the house very popular until the Lord Chamberlain interposed to prohibit the caricature. *The Wedding March* was a semi-musical rendering of the immortal *Chapeau de Paille d'Italie*. Retiring from the management—to which, however, for a brief while, she returned—Miss Litton left the conduct of affairs to Mr. John Hare. On the 13th March, 1875, ten years after the opening of the Prince of Wales's, Mr. Hare's management began. It was the second important step to the liberation of the stage from its long worn trammels. How directly it sprang from the previous experiments is at once evident. During the Bancroft management, so soon as it was well established, Mr. Hare became as it were Mr. Bancroft's lieutenant. In the entire season of Robertsonian comedy he had a part as important as that of his captain. What sort of characters each of the three principal actors would be allotted was one of the delightful problems, the solution of which led literary and artistic London to a first night performance at the Prince of Wales's. Magnificently did Mr. Hare fulfil the functions assigned him, and his rise to the front of his profession may count among the most rapid ever accomplished. In *Society* there were four principal parts—the MAUD HETHERINGTON, sparkling and winsome of Miss Marie Wilton, the JOHN CHODD, arrogant in vulgarity of John Clarke, the SYDNEY DARYLL of Mr. Bancroft, the first of a series of admirable sketches of social life, and the LORD PTARMIGANT of Mr. Hare. In its way the last was the freshest and most amusing of all; and the figure of the irritable, petulant, somnolent old nobleman proved in itself enough to build up a reputation. To the MARY NETLEY of Mrs. Bancroft and the ANGUS MCALISTER of his manager Mr. Hare responded with PRINCE PEROVSKY, another wonderful picture of aristocratic manners. A complete change of front took place on the famous production of *Caste*, the whilom representative of noblemen and diplomats giving a startlingly realistic and life-like presentation of a working man. A performance more humorous and artistic than that of the amorous gasfitter has rarely stirred London or revealed so unexpectedly the genius and range of an actor. This character, and the bibulous vapourings of George Honey as Eccles, did as much to raise the piece to the popularity it enjoyed for a quarter of a century as the domestic interest divinely shown by Mrs. Bancroft and Miss Lydia Foote. The Hon. Bruce Fanquhere of *Play*, the Beau Farintosh of *School*, and the Duncombe Duncombe of *M.P.*, were three successive triumphs diversified in character but alike as specimens of high comedy. With these Robertsonian parts had to be associated Sir John Vesey ("Stingy Jack") in *Money*, and Sir Peter Teazle in *The School for Scandal*.

In undertaking the management of the Court Mr. Hare was unable to catch another Robertson, though he cast his nets wide in the effort. His early experiments accordingly, though not wanting in intelligence, were not specially remunerative; and though he opened his season as the DUC DE CHAVANNES in Charles Coghlan's *Lady Flora* he did not always appear in the pieces he produced, showing in this respect a species of reticence and self-denial almost unique in his profession, and not invariably judicious and commendable. Perhaps the most distinguished feature in his management was his production of *Olivia*, Mr. Wills's version of *The Vicar of Wakefield*, in which he entrusted DR. PRIMROSE—a part he might well have himself assumed—to Mr. Vezin, and OLIVIA to Miss Terry, he himself having no share in the performance beyond management. Of the more ambitious pieces he gave, Mr. Gilbert's *Broken Hearts*, *The Queen's Shilling* of Mr. Godfrey, and a *Scrap of Paper* (*Les Pattes de Mouche*), in which he was COLONEL DAUNT, are the best remembered. Mr. Hamilton Aïdé's *Nine Days' Wonder* and Mr. Coghlan's *Brothers* are also recalled, but Lord Lytton's *House of Darnley*, on which some hopes had been built, is entirely forgotten. A revival of *New Men and Old Acres*, and one of *The Ladies' Battle*, proved judicious, and *A Quiet Rubber*, an adaptation of *Une Partie de Piquet*, was a triumph, enriching the stage with the part of LORD KILCLARE,

THE STAGE IN THE YEAR 1900: A SOUVENIR.

one of the most touching and the best remembered in Mr. Hare's repertory. During this period of management Mr. Hare had the inestimable advantage of including in his company Mr. and Mrs. Kendal, his subsequent partners in the management of the St. James's. Good fortune did not take flight from the Court with the departure of Mr. Hare. Mr. Godfrey's *Parvenu* ranked as one of the most popular pieces of the day, and Mr. Pinero gave *The Rector*, one of the earliest of his efforts in light comedy. He had been preceded at the same house by his great rival, Mr. Henry Arthur Jones having already exhibited there a one-act comedietta, *A Clerical Error*. Though but a duologue, *My Milliner's Bill*, by Godfrey, attracted much attention. Then came the marvellous series of farces by Mr. Pinero, produced by Arthur Cecil and John Clayton, enough in themselves to establish the fortunes of the theatre—*The Magistrate*, *The School Mistress*, and the enchanting *Dandy Dick*, a piece breathing the very spirit of fun, and acted to perfection. When the house was demolished and re-erected on the other side of Sloane Square, fortune clung to it for a while. Under the management first of Mrs. John Wood and Mr. Arthur Chudleigh, and then of Mr.

Chudleigh alone, were produced *The Weaker Sex* and *The Amazons*, delightful pieces of Mr. Pinero, and *A White Lie*, by Mr. Sydney Grundy. The line of dramatic progression has been unbroken. *Trelawney of the Wells*, another of Mr. Pinero's brilliant farces, has only given way to *His Excellency the Governor* and *A Royal Marriage*, two of the most inspiriting of modern works, by Captain Marshall, and *Wheels within Wheels*, by Mr. R. C. Carton. Many other pieces, from the *White Pilgrim* of Mr. Herman Merivale, given at the old house, to *A Bit of Old Chelsea* by Mrs. Beringer, deserve mention in connection with a theatre which—though once or twice discouragingly and, as it appeared, wantonly mismanaged—has, until a year ago, held its head well above water, and has not seldom stood in the very front rank of popularity.

CHAPTER IV.

WE have now come to a point at which the enumeration of new theatres may be suspended, and a glance taken at the proceedings of other and long established houses. By the time that the Hare and Kendal management was established at the St. James's a degree of excellence in regard to cast and *mise en scène* had been reached which, though it has since been maintained, has not at home or abroad been surpassed. Fifteen years of intelligent observation upon the part of certain actors, and energy and resolution upon that of others, had raised the London stage to a pitch of equality in this respect with that of Berlin, Vienna, or Paris. While attributing to the influence of the Bancroft management and its followers and successors the genesis of this revival, sight must not be lost of the fact that the movement was carried out by many who were subject to no influence of the kind. The figure of

Henry Irving stands conspicuous and august as an example of this. His fair and gracious associate in many of his triumphs had had a portion of her experience at the Prince of Wales's, and might possibly form a sort of connecting link between two schools, if such they can be called. Sir Henry's training had been wholly different. Not indeed until he had become his own manager was his influence upon the stage fully developed. Many fine performances had been given by him at the Princess's, the St. James's, the Vaudeville and the Queen's, and the public had come to look upon the young comedian as one from whom the highest things might in time be anticipated. When, however, in 1871 Bateman took the Lyceum with the view of exploiting his daughter Isabel rather than the great actor whose services he had almost unconsciously secured, and produced on the 11th September, 1871, *Fanchetta*, a conventional rendering of *La Petite Fadette* of George Sand, the failure of his experiment seemed more than probable. When in 1872 Irving appeared as MATHIAS in *The Bells*, and electrified the public as it had not been electrified since the days of Robson, the fact that one of the greatest of actors had dawned upon the world was scarcely recognised.

THE STAGE IN THE YEAR 1900: A SOUVENIR.

It was indeed hardly evident. A wonderfully fine and powerful impersonation was contemplated and the psychological significance of the study was granted. The character was not, however, charged with all the significance it subsequently carried, and it did not, and still does not, reveal the greatest gifts of the actor. These were soon to be disclosed. *Raising the Wind* showed the more diverting aspects of Irving's comic method without adding greatly to his fame. Much the same may be said about *Eugene Aram*, another strange and morbid, though fascinating study. Before the production of this, however, Wills's *Charles I* had revealed another higher and more poetical phase of Irving's gifts, and elicited a homage of tears such as has rarely been accorded.

Recollections of the earliest performance of *Charles I* were swallowed up in those of subsequent and even more admirable performances of the same play, when the marvellous temperament and disciplined art of Miss Ellen Terry replaced the pensive prettiness of Miss Isabel Bateman. By this time, though greater triumphs were in store, the Lyceum had become the most representative English home of the poetical and imaginative drama, and counted as one of the houses at which the aid of the sister arts was called in to enhance the attractions of the spectacle. The mounting of *Charles I* was signal in beauty, and the view of the monarch with his queen and family floating among the water-lilies of the Thames survives in the recollection as well as in Mr. Margetson's picture. Following this great triumph came a revival of Lord Lytton's *Richelieu* and the production of Mr. Hamilton Aidé's powerful if theatrical *Philip*. Then came what was at once the greatest triumph of the Bateman management and the most inspired accomplishment of Mr. Irving's genius. The run of a couple of hundred nights of *Hamlet* was of course at the time unprecedented. There is finality neither in art nor in ambition, and long runs in *Hamlet* have since been rigorously exacted. That all of these have proved so remunerative as did the first has not been asserted. Subsequent HAMLETS have contested with Irving the supremacy, and Mr. Wilson Barrett, Mr. Tree and Mr. Forbes-Robertson still find their admirers, upholders and worshippers. Each succeeding HAMLET has been careful to provide himself with a picturesque and poetical environment. At the time the Lyceum *mise en scène* won general recognition, which extended even to foreign countries;

and those in France most justified in speaking with authority wrote in high eulogy of the marvels which had been accomplished.

Hamlet was followed by *Macbeth*, with Miss Bateman as LADY MACBETH, and *Othello*, neither of which attained equal popularity, and the great actor then repeated a performance of DORICOURT in *The Belle's Stratagem*, in which he had been seen with Miss Herbert. *Richard III*, played almost for the first time since the Restoration in Shakespeare's text as distinguished from Colley Cibber's, gave the actor's powers of humour and sarcasm their full opportunity, and ranked as one of his finest Shakespearian interpretations. It had been preceded by Tennyson's *Queen Mary*—in which Irving gave a superb picture of the cold-blooded, ambitious and bigoted Philip, and Miss Bateman came forward to present the defeated, amorous and hysterical Queen—and was followed by *The Lyons Mail*, with the fine and deeply contrasted dual character LESURQUES and DUBOSC. One more of the actor's grimmest, subtlest and deadliest impersonations was supplied in LOUIS XI, in which the closest comparisons were challenged with Charles Kean. Louis XI was a wonderful conception, in the elaboration of which the actor had good support from Mrs. Chippendale, Mr. Fernandez and Mr. Cartwright.

After playing VANDERDECKEN in a drama of W. G. Wills and Mr. Percy Fitzgerald, and reappearing as JINGLE, Irving on the 17th April, 1879, celebrated the opening of his management of the Lyceum by the engagement of Miss Ellen Terry, who has since been his all but constant companion. Her first appearance was made as PAULINE in *The Lady of Lyons*, a lovely performance, which had previously been seen and has rarely been surpassed. Mr. Kyrle Bellew joined the company as GLAVIS. In *jeune premier* parts, CLAUDE MELNOTTE, ROMEO, and the like, Irving never reached the same height as he did in those which demanded a higher and more imperial order of talents. A hurried account of the Irving management of the Lyceum would occupy in itself a volume. The most salient features alone can be mentioned. Irving's SIR EDWARD MORTIMER in *The Iron Chest* attracted comparatively little attention; his SHYLOCK in *The Merchant of Venice* excited a polemic. Miss Ellen Terry's PORTIA was established in public reputation as the most poetical and imaginative that was within public recollection. It

THE STAGE IN THE YEAR 1900: A SOUVENIR.

was, it may be maintained, the most beautiful that had been given. In the Casket scene a vision of dream-like beauty and perfume was realised, and the great scene of the fourth act was played in a style that the present generation has not seen equalled. Irving's SHYLOCK meantime rose to the height of popularity. It was the vindication of a race, almost indeed the vindication of humanity, and it displayed with marvellous force and intensity a range of the highest gifts. How far it answers to the conception of Shakespeare is a question not now to be fully discussed. The fifth act was after a while omitted, a proceeding necessary if the piece is to be a tragedy instead of a comedy—a modern heresy always to be combated. The delicious framework of love, music and poetry in which the story is enshrined tells what was Shakespeare's view of the subject. The Venetian pictures of this piece revealed English stage resources at their best, and eclipsed anything that foreign management had exhibited.

A triumph for Miss Terry in *Iolanthe*, otherwise *King René's Daughter*,* was followed by one even more remarkable for her associate in *The Corsican Brothers*, in which she did not appear. Irving's

* Wills's version at the Lyceum was called *Iolanthe*, but Miss Faucit, Mrs. Stirling and *others had been seen in previous adaptations called King René's Daughter.*

fine presentation of the brothers DEI FRANCHI greatly impressed the playgoer. William Terriss joined the company, appearing as CHÂTEAU RENAUD. *The Cup*, by Lord Tennyson, was a noble and praiseworthy production, which inspired the public rather by the magical beauty of its pagan ceremonial, the mystic rites of the Ephesian Artemis, than by the merits of poetry and acting, noteworthy as these were. A revival of *Othello* on the 2nd May, 1881, with Edwin Booth as the MOOR, Irving as IAGO, Terriss as CASSIO, Mead as BRABANTIO, Mr. Pinero as RODERIGO, Miss Pauncefote as EMILIA, and Miss Terry as DESDEMONA, constituted one of the greatest treats offered to the playgoing world.

In a revival of *The Two Roses* Irving reappeared as DIGBY GRANT, and David James as "Our" MR. JENKINS, while Miss Winifred Emery was LOTTIE and Mr. Alexander made his first appearance in London as CALEB DEECIE. The revival was gratifying, but the piece had aged. *Romeo and Juliet* in the beauty of its scenery eclipsed all memories of *The Merchant of Venice*, or indeed of all previous representations. Some few memorable impersonations were given, including the NURSE of Mrs.

THE STAGE IN THE YEAR 1900: A SOUVENIR.

Stirling, but the memories of the piece were swallowed up in those of *Much Ado about Nothing* which followed. Miss Ellen Terry's BEATRICE and Irving's BENEDICK were alike inimitable, and the DON PEDRO of Mr. Terriss, Mr. Glenney's DON JOHN, Mr. Forbes-Robertson's CLAUDIO, Mr. Fernandez's LEONATO, Mr. Howe's ANTONIO, and Miss Millward's HERO, were portions of a not to be forgotten cast. *Robert Macaire* was first given for a charity with a cast such as can rarely be obtained except for a single occasion, comprising Miss Ada Cavendish and Mrs. Bancroft, together with Mr. Toole as JACQUES STROP. *Twelfth Night* was played in order that admirers of Irving might see him as MALVOLIO, a part eminently suited to some of his special gifts; Mr. Fred Terry was SEBASTIAN, the resemblance between him and VIOLA, played by Miss Ellen Terry, being naturally effective. After a revival of *Olivia*—in which Miss Terry was OLIVIA and Miss Winifred Emery SOPHIA, Terriss an absolutely unsurpassed SQUIRE THORNHILL, and Irving a most touching DR. PRIMROSE—there came Mr. Wills's adaptation of *Faust*. Sticklers for the old censured the production as wanting in many respects. It was, however, singularly beautiful. Irving's MEPHISTOPHELES is the best to be recalled on the dramatic or the lyric stage; the mingled humour and cynicism were irresistible. Whatever criticism may say, it is impossible to resist the conviction that Goethe would have been enchanted with instances of such ideal interpretation as were furnished in the MEPHISTOPHELES and the GRETCHEN. FAUST found a very handsome representative in "Harry" Conway, and Mr. Alexander was a picturesque VALENTINE. The scenes in front of the church in Nuremburg were of great beauty, and the Brocken revels were beyond anything that had then been done in depicting infernal proceedings. The apotheosis of GRETCHEN was beautiful and effective. There are those who doubt whether the Lyceum management ever reached a point higher as regards interpretation and environment than was on this occasion attained. *The Dead Heart*—with Irving as ROBERT LANDRY, Webster's greatest part, Sir Squire Bancroft as L'ABBÉ LATOUR, Arthur Stirling as LEGRAND, Miss Kate Phillips as CERISETTE, and Miss Ellen Terry as CATHERINE DUVAL—preceded *Ravenswood*, Mr. Herman Merivale's adaptation of Scott's *Bride of Lammermoor*, a hyperborean *Romeo and Juliet*, the mystery, fatefulness and passion of which were divinely expressed, and the famous revival of *Henry VIII*, well remembered features in which, besides the CARDINAL WOLSEY of Irving and the QUEEN KATHARINE of Miss Terry, were the KING of Mr. Terriss, the BUCKINGHAM of Mr. Forbes-Robertson, in all respects a masterpiece, the CARDINAL CAMPEIUS of Mr. Beaumont, the LORD SANDS of Mr. Gilbert Farquhar, and the ANNE BULLEN of Miss Violet Vanbrugh. *King Lear*, with Irving as the KING, Mr. Terriss as EDGAR, Mr. Frank Cooper as EDMUND, and Miss Terry as CORDELIA, came next, and then, on the 6th February, 1893, came a crowning triumph of the management, Tennyson's *Becket*. It may be maintained that this is the finest performance of historical tragedy the present generation has witnessed. If it were sought to show what in the art of Sir Henry Irving is most imaginative, most creative, most solemn, and most inspired, his presentation of the ambitious and heroic Cardinal Chancellor would by general consent be taken. Splendid, picturesque and noble in bearing the figure stood, tragic in dignity and in suffering. The diction was perfect in harmony, and not a trace of elocutionary heresy or mannerism with which the actor had been rebuked was to be detected. Miss Ellen Terry was, of course, the

Rosamund, Miss Geneviève Ward was Eleanor of Aquitaine, and Miss Kate Phillips Margery. The splendidly gallant and impetuous Henry II of Mr. Terriss is not to be forgotten, and the priests and knights of the court might almost merit a separate mention. Two more characters belong to this period of supreme triumph, Corporal Gregory Brewster in Dr. Conan Doyle's *Story of Waterloo*, and King Arthur in Mr. Carr's dramatisation of Tennyson's poem. The former study may be classed with the best remembered masterpieces of acting, with Daddy Hardacre by Robson, Rip Van Winkle by Jefferson, and Noel in *La Joie fait Peur* by Regnier. The much lauded Cyrano of M. Coquelin does not come within measurable distance of these.

It seemed as if the entire careers of Irving and Miss Terry had fitted them to play King Arthur and Queen Guenevere. The representation had accordingly signal beauty. Mr. Forbes-Robertson was a typical Sir Lancelot, and might have been a still more typical Gawaine had another phase of the great representative legend been taken. Miss Lena Ashwell as Elaine seemed born to play the "lily maid of Astolat," Miss Geneviève Ward was Morgan le Fay, and Messrs. Cooper, Mellish,

THE STAGE IN THE YEAR 1900: A SOUVENIR.

Hague, Tyars, Valentine, Julius Knight and Martin Harvey gave striking representations of the Knights of the Round Table, Arthur's associates. A performance by Irving of *Don Quixote* also demands record, as does the presentation of *Cymbeline*, which, as arranged by Sir Henry Irving, had many splendid and interesting features, among them being the IMOGEN of Miss Terry, Sir Henry's IACHIMO, Mr. Macklin's CYMBELINE, the CLOTEN of Mr. Norman Forbes, and the POSTHUMUS of Mr. Frank Cooper.

Other novelties consisted of *Peter the Great*, by Mr. Laurence Irving; *The Medicine Man*, by H. D. Traill and Mr. Robert S. Hichens; and two pieces from the French, *Madame Sans-Gêne* and *Robespierre*, which, though finely acted, scarcely kept up the highest traditions of the house. Mr. Calmour's *Amber Heart* should be remembered as furnishing Miss Terry with a part in which her poetical gifts were of highest service. A revival, for a benefit, of *Werner* should not be overlooked.

Many intercalary seasons at the Lyceum have to be noted, and one or two of these will in due course come in for comment. The brilliant but short career of Miss Mary Anderson belongs entirely to the Lyceum, at which house the actress was originally seen on the 1st September, 1883, as PARTHENIA in *Ingomar*, a play by Mrs. Maria Anne Lovell, produced at Drury Lane in 1851, and so belonging entirely to the Victorian epoch. It is a translation from the Baron von Munch Bellinghausen, otherwise Frederick Halm, and was produced by James Anderson—an almost solitary success of his ill-starred management of Drury Lane—Anderson playing INGOMAR and Miss Vandenhoff PARTHENIA. On Miss Anderson's revival the INGOMAR was Mr. J. H. Barnes. Endowed with little experience, but with a sylph-like and willowy figure, a well-shaped head ravishingly set on a graceful neck, and with beautiful and luminous brows, Miss Anderson was probably the best looking of the many women whose stage success has depended largely on their reputation for beauty. PAULINE in *The Lady of Lyons*, and GALATEA in *Pygmalion and Galatea*, followed, the latter performance eliciting from Mr. Gilbert the utterance that he considered Miss Anderson's conception of GALATEA to be artistically more beautiful, but dramatically less effective, than that of Mrs. Kendal, the original exponent. For Miss Anderson Mr. Gilbert wrote *Comedy and Tragedy*, recently revived at the Comedy by Miss Janette Steer. As CLARICE in this play Miss Anderson had the support of Mr. Barnes and Mr. Alexander. An exquisitely beautiful JULIET, she yet made no such impression as had been caused by Stella Colas, Miss Neilson, and Miss Ellen Terry. JULIET may indeed be considered the weakest performance she gave. Her JULIA in *The Hunchback* had good passages, and her ROSALIND had admirable grace and a measure of intuition. In a revival of *The Winter's Tale* Miss Anderson made a bold innovation by doubling the parts of HERMIONE and PERDITA, a proceeding frequently challenged but on the whole justified. As is too often the case with American actresses, she made sad havoc of Shakespeare's text, chiefly, but not wholly, in an effort at expurgation. There was much that was beautiful in her performance of PERDITA, and the dance which she led off was the most exquisite thing in its class ever realised on the modern stage. It was the very poetry, joy and beauty of motion. Upon her marriage the actress permanently quitted the stage.

CHAPTER V.

The English stage had long before this time regained all, and more than all, its old ascendancy over the public and resumed its place in the brotherhood of arts. When a new production was mounted at a leading theatre, painters of the highest renown lent their aid in designing scenery and costumes, and composers of eminence contributed incidental music. The portraits of principal actors were once more exhibited on the walls of the Royal Academy; while two of the most celebrated of their number—Mr. Henry Irving and Mr. Squire Bancroft—were selected for the honour of knighthood, establishing thus a precedent for distinctions to which previously the stage had scarcely aspired.

In noticing the influence upon this advance of newly-erected theatres, injustice must not be done to other and older houses which recognised the

need of advance and took part in the triumphal
procession. The theatres catering for the general
public were the slowest to move, and came as the
rearguard rather than the vanguard of the army
of progress. Since the memorable declaration of
Chatterton, the manager of Drury Lane, that
" Shakespeare spelt ruin and Byron bankruptcy "—
an assertion accurate enough in the period of his
own cheeseparing mismanagement—the sluggish blood
of old Drury had felt some promptings of the spring.
Transmitted by Phelps, a sound and an admirable comedian but a conventional and hidebound
tragedian, the traditions of tragedy derived from
Macready and Charles Kean, and by them from the
Kembles, had fallen into disrepute and become a
byword to the cultivated. Something else had to be
found to take the place of tragedy. That something
was naturally melodrama—picturesque, romantic,
spectacular, sensational. Every variety was tried in
turn, though the results were seldom remunerative,
and at the end of the year Drury Lane had to
depend as a rule upon its pantomime for a small
balance, if such, on any terms, could be obtained.

The question of opera stands, of course, apart.
The first speculation in melodrama of Chatterton

when disassociated from his former partner, Falconer, was in 1868, in Halliday's *Great City*, a poor piece even in its poor class. Adaptations from Scott marked a higher effort, and Miss Neilson as REBECCA in *Ivanhoe* and AMY ROBSART in *Kenilworth* attracted others beside Chatterton's customary patrons. *The King o' Scots*, with Phelps doubling the parts of KING JAMES and TRAPBOIS, the miser, was a sustained and well-merited success. Chatterton, however, went the way of most of his predecessors, and with little aid from Shakespeare and less from Byron "spelt" bankruptcy on his own account, retiring with heavy liabilities which he was unable to meet.

His departure made room for Sir Augustus Harris, an inspired organiser, who could lay his hand almost always on the right piece and the right man, and who raised the fortunes of the house to the highest pitch, and dying prematurely left behind him, like a great captain, lieutenants, notably Mr. Arthur Collins, able to carry out his schemes. On the 6th November, 1879, Harris began the management of what has been miscalled, so far as modern days are concerned, the national theatre, and signalised his entry upon his functions by producing in the following July *The World*, in the arrangement of which he allied himself with Paul Meritt and Henry Pettitt. *Youth*, the novelty of 1881, was by Meritt and Harris. *Pluck*, in 1882, was by Harris and Pettitt. An autumn drama and a pantomime were Harris's general, though not invariable, programme, the house being let during the remainder of the year for opera, English or foreign, German or Italian. *A Sailor and his Lass*, in 1883, was by Harris and Mr. Robert Buchanan. *Human Nature*, by Pettitt and Harris, followed in 1885; *A Run of Luck*, by the same, in 1886; *Pleasure*, by Harris and Meritt, in 1887. In *The Armada*, in which an appeal was made in 1888 to national sentiment, and in *The Royal Oak*, 1889, Harris collaborated with Mr. Henry Hamilton. Pettitt's name reappeared in 1890 with that of Harris in *A Million of Money*, and stood alone in 1891 in *A Sailor's Knot*. *The Prodigal Daughter*, in 1892, was by Harris and Pettitt, as was *A Life of Pleasure* in 1893. Mr. Cecil Raleigh, associated in 1894 with Harris and Mr. Henry Hamilton, is responsible for *The Derby Winner*, and the same combination gave the stage in 1895 *Cheer, Boys, Cheer*. Harris did not long survive his old associate Pettitt, but died in 1896, in which year there was no autumn drama. *The White Heather*, in 1897, was by Mr. Raleigh and Mr. Hamilton, as was *The Great Ruby* the following year. *Hearts are Trumps*, in 1899, was by Mr. Raleigh alone, as was in 1900 *The Price of Peace*, in its class the greatest triumph the house has known.

While widely different in story, these pieces were so far alike that they aimed at supplying pictures of the actual world in the midst of which we live, and associating the interest with sensational incidents sometimes of a sufficiently thrilling kind. Not the highest order of drama are these things, but they are the best in their line. On them and on the pantomimes prodigious sums are lavished, and the latest discoveries of science are exhausted in their production. When we hear of the dresses first seen at a conspicuous social and aristocratic *fête* being worn by actresses and supernumeraries, the thought goes back to the time when Stuart or Hanoverian royalty or nobility graced some favourite actors with dresses that had been worn on State occasions, and even, it is whispered, at coronations.

It is impossible to indicate a tithe of those taking part in the later productions at Drury Lane. Among them may be mentioned the Vokes family,

THE STAGE IN THE YEAR 1900: A SOUVENIR.

the brightest pantomimists old Drury had seen, whose reign covered the seventies and a portion of the eighties, and who, in addition to their saltatory gifts, were distinguished both as vocalists and comedians. They gave as a family many successful pieces, half plays, half entertainments, and Miss Rosina Vokes (Mrs. Cecil Clay), an eminently vivacious actress, was, until just before her death, at the head of a clever and popular company. In some few pieces Harris himself took part, though he soon withdrew. William Rignold, Miss Fanny Brough, Miss Fanny Josephs, Miss Helen Barry, Miss Caroline Hill, Mrs. Billington, Mr. W. H. Vernon, Mr. Harry Nicholls, Mr. J. H. Barnes, Mr. Arthur Dacre, Miss Lydia Foote, Mr. J. G. Grahame, and Mr. Edmund Leathes, were all associated with the house. A list of subsequent performers would constitute a mere nomenclature. Best remembered and, in themselves, best worth remembering, are the performances given at Drury Lane in recent days by artists such as Mrs. John Wood, Mrs. Cecil Raleigh, Miss Beatrice Lamb, Miss Eleanor Calhoun, Miss Kate Rorke, Miss Mary Brough, and Messrs. H. Neville, Arthur Bourchier, C. M. Lowne, Charles Cartwright, Eversfield and Loraine. Proof of the popularity, if not of the merit, of plays and performances is furnished in the fact that many outlasted the season at Drury Lane and were revived in the following year, or carried to complete their run at the Princess's or the Olympic.

With Drury Lane as popular houses may be associated in the past the Adelphi, the Princess's and the Olympic. It is a curious and significant fact that at these three houses the reign of melodrama seems to be over, handicapped as they are by the opportunities furnished by the huge stage of Drury Lane and the lavish scale on which spectacles can there be produced.

The Adelphi seems to have abandoned all notion of rivalry with Drury Lane, while the Princess's (recent experiments at which have relegated it to the position of an outlying house) is, it seems, to be turned into a music hall, and the Olympic, for reasons independent of the character of the entertainment produced, is doomed to speedy destruction.

In early days the Adelphi was perhaps the most formidable rival of the patent houses. At the outset of the Victorian era it challenged supremacy with the Haymarket. With the production in 1821 of Moncrieff's *Tom and Jerry*, with Wrench as CORINTHIAN TOM,

Watkins Burroughs as JERRY HAWTHORNE, Keeley as JESSAMY GREEN, and Mrs. Waylett as SUE, it anticipated by half a century a class of pieces, beginning with *Formosa*, which attracted the present generation to Drury Lane. Of a worthier class was *The Pilot*, from Fenimore Cooper, with Terry, the friend of Sir Walter Scott, as the PILOT, Yates as BARNSTABLE, John Reeve as BOROUGHCLIFFE, and T. P. Cooke as LONG TOM COFFIN. Terry retired from the management ruined, and Charles Mathews the elder joined Yates. This was the period of *The Black Vulture*, Buckstone's *Wreck Ashore*, *Henrietta the Forsaken*, *Victorine*, *Isabell*, and innumerable pieces of various authors, in which Mrs. Yates, Mrs. Honey, Mrs. Nisbett and Ben Webster were seen to advantage. T. D. Rice popularised JIM CROW. *Nicholas Nickleby*, with Yates as MANTALINI, O. Smith as NEWMAN NOGGS, Wilkinson as SQUEERS, and Mrs. Keeley as SMIKE, was followed by *Oliver Twist*, including many of the same actors, and by the appearance of Hackett in *Rip Van Winkle*. The management of Webster and Madame Celeste showed the latter as MIAMI, and Wright and Paul Bedford as "MUSTER" GRINNIDGE and JACK GONG, in Buckstone's *Green Bushes*. *Belphegor* and *Janet Pride* belonged to succeeding days.

THE STAGE IN THE YEAR 1900: A SOUVENIR.

The new theatre, opened in 1858, welcomed Mr. Toole to a home at which he had for a constant associate Miss Woolgar (Mrs. Alfred Mellon). Webster, in *The Dead Heart*, made way for Mr. and Mrs. Boucicault in *The Colleen Bawn*, which was followed by *The Octoroon*, Miss Bateman came out in *Leah*, Mr. Toole appeared as PAUL PRY, and Mr. Jefferson played his immortal part of RIP VAN WINKLE. Among other novelties, the most remarkable was *No Thoroughfare*, by Dickens and Wilkie Collins, with Fechter as OBENREIZER and Webster as JOEY LADLE. Since that time dramas by Messrs. Byron, Sims, Pettitt, Buchanan, Haddon Chambers, Comyns Carr, B. C. Stephenson and Clement Scott have brought before the public many actors, English and American, without destroying the character of the Adelphi as a popular house. *In the Ranks*, by Messrs. Sims and Pettitt, gave Mr. Warner some opportunities on which he seized. Mr. Terriss and Miss Millward, until the unfortunate death of the former by the knife of an assassin, were main supports of the theatre. Here some of the most picturesque performances of the former were given, notably his WILLIAM in *Black Eyed Susan*, and his presentation in *One of the Best*, by Messrs. Seymour

THE STAGE IN THE YEAR 1900: A SOUVENIR.

Hicks and George Edwardes, of an officer unjustly convicted, who is stripped of his medals and the insignia of his grade, an idea which is of course derived from a French *cause célèbre*. *Secret Service*, the best play produced in recent years at the Adelphi, is of American extraction. As it was given by an English as well as an American company mention of it is justifiable.

Not until long past the middle of the century did the Princess's come to rank as a popular house. Its early successes were in music, and it might almost have been regarded as an opera house. It subsequently saw Edwin Forrest and Miss Cushman as MACBETH and LADY MACBETH, and Macready and Leigh Murray as HAMLET and LAERTES. Here Macready in 1846 made his appearance as the KING in *The King of the Commons*, a once celebrated piece by the Rev. J. White, and here the following year he enacted for the first time PHILIP VAN ARTEVELDE in Sir Henry Taylor's drama. The memorable management of Charles Kean and Robert Keeley began in August, 1850, and, though Keeley soon seceded, the theatre under Charles Kean witnessed many memorable revivals of Shakespeare and Byron, together with the production of *The Corsican Brothers*,

Faust and Marguerite, *Louis XI*, and plays by Westland Marston, Douglas Jerrold, Boucicault, Charles Reade, Slous, Palgrave Simpson and others. Among those taking part in the various revivals and novelties were Charles Kean and his wife, the Wigans, Keeleys, Walter Lacy, Bartley, Addison, Drinkwater Meadows, Ryder, Harley, Miss Heath, Miss Bufton, Miss Poole, Miss Kate Terry, and Miss Chapman. In 1859 the theatre passed into the hands of Augustus Harris, the elder, who produced Oxenford's adaptation, *Ivy Hall*, in which Irving made his first appearance in London. On the 27th October, 1860, Fechter appeared in *Ruy Blas*. His *Don Cæsar de Bazan* followed 11th February, 1861, *Hamlet* on the 20th March, and his *Othello* on 23rd October. Brushing away the cobwebs of ignorant and irreverent tradition, Fechter's HAMLET gave rise to a fierce polemic, but was in the main approved. It was otherwise with his OTHELLO, which was no less generally condemned. Fechter's IAGO to the OTHELLO of Ryder was, however, a success. Almost the only serious defect in the HAMLET was that it presented the Prince as a sentimental *jeune premier* with almost a suggestion of Don Juan Tenorio. Experiments of interest were Walter Montgomery's

THE STAGE IN THE YEAR 1900: A SOUVENIR.

OTHELLO and the JULIET of Stella Colas, the latter a performance of much beauty. The Webb brothers appeared as the DROMIOS in *The Comedy of Errors*, Mr. Hermann Vezin gave a superb rendering of Wills's *Man of Airlie*, and Boucicault obtained a triumph with his *Arrah na Pogue*. Reade's *Never Too Late to Mend* had a success of scandal, and *The Huguenot Captain* of Watts Phillips introduced Miss Neilson to a theatre at which she did not long remain. Mention may be made of Marston's *Donna Diana*, with Mr. and Mrs. Vezin as the hero and heroine, and George Vining as the *gracioso;* the revival of *True to the Core*, the drama which carried off the prize offered for the best English nautical play (it had been first given at the Surrey); *Barnaby Rudge*, with Mrs. John Wood as MISS MIGGS; and Robertson's failure, *Shadow Tree Shaft*. One management succeeded another, a memorable performance being Charles Warner's COUPEAU in *Drink*, Charles Reade's adaptation of *L'Assommoir*.

The Silver King of Mr. Henry Arthur Jones and the late Henry Herman won recognition as the best melodrama of its day, and opened out for the Princess management—now in the hands of Mr. Wilson Barrett—a period of all but unprecedented popularity. Mr. Barrett himself as WILFRED DENVER (the Silver King), Miss Eastlake, his constant associate, as the heroine, Mr. Willard as SKINNER, and Mr. George Barrett as JAIKES, a faithful servant, commended piece and management to public approval. Mr. Barrett also appeared as JACK HEARNE in *The Romany Rye* of Mr. George R. Sims. CLAUDIAN in the *Claudian* of Messrs. Wills and Herman followed, and was in turn succeeded by the *Chatterton* of Mr. Henry Arthur Jones and Herman, a play in which Mr. Barrett showed his best gifts, and one which won the praise of men such as Matthew Arnold and John Ruskin. Mr. Barrett's *Hamlet*, which was played for the due number of nights, had many picturesque and elocutionary qualities, but was marred by some curiously fantastical readings. *Junius, or the Household Gods*, of Lord Lytton, played in 1885, was a reactionary and not wholly satisfactory experiment. In *Hoodman Blind*, and again in *The Lord Harry*, Mr. Wilson Barrett's name was associated in authorship with that of Mr. Henry Arthur Jones. *Clito*, a tragedy in verse, by Mr. Sydney Grundy, showed Mr. Barrett in one of the classical parts in which his soul delights. *Ben-my-Chree*, produced 17th May, 1888, was a fruit of the happy association between Mr. Wilson Barrett and Mr. Hall Caine. *Nowadays, a Tale of the Turf*, was by Mr. Barrett alone. Other performances of the actor are associated with various houses—*The Sign of the Cross* being remembered in connection with the Lyric and the Lyceum. Since the management of the Princess's came into other hands it has known one triumph of good alloy in *Two Little Vagabonds*, adapted by Messrs. G. R. Sims and Arthur Shirley from *Les Deux Gosses* of M. Pierre Decourcelle, and produced on the 23rd September, 1896; a well constructed and a pathetic piece, which received a capital interpretation from Misses Sydney Fairbrother and Kate Tyndall, and Messrs. Ernest Leicester and Edmund Gurney.

With an existence dating back to the beginning of the century, the Olympic began to have a history when it came under the management of Madame Vestris, who produced and acted in the sprightly burlesques of Planché and Dance. It was long a home for fashionable levities, and had a company admirably trained to act in such The tragic performances of G. V. Brooke, the best English OTHELLO, took place thereat about the middle of the century. Managements of William Farren and

Alfred Wigan further commended the Olympic, where also Brooke and Miss Helen Faucit appeared in Westland Marston's *Philip of France*. In 1853 Robson appeared at the Olympic for the first time. At this house his short and brilliant career was practically passed. Here he was seen as DADDY HARDACRE, as SAMPSON BURR in *The Porter's Knot*, as PETER PROBITY in *The Chimney Corner*, as DESMARETS in *Plot and Passion*, as JOB WORT in *A Blighted Being*, in burlesques of Brough and of Talfourd, and in the immortal *Yellow Dwarf*. At the time of his death, in 1864, though he had for some time ceased to act, he was part-manager of the theatre. In later years the house was associated with Mr. Henry Neville, who was seen here as BOB BRIERLY in *The Ticket of Leave Man*, and in many of his most admirable and popular characters. Sam Emery is remembered as DANIEL PEGGOTTY in *Little Em'ly*; Miss Kate Terry was seen in *Henry Dunbar*, in *A Wolf in Sheep's Clothing*, and in many beautifully interpreted parts. Miss Ada Cavendish gave at the Olympic—of which she was for some time manager —MERCY MERRICK in *The New Magdalen* of Wilkie Collins. She then played JULIET, MADONNA PIA in Westland Marston's *Put to the Test*, and LADY

THE STAGE IN THE YEAR 1900: A SOUVENIR.

CLANCARTY in Taylor's *Lady Clancarty*, in which Mr. Neville was LORD CLANCARTY, Mr. Charles Neville, and afterwards Mr. Charles Sugden, WILLIAM III, Mr. Vernon LORD CHARLES SPENCER, and Miss Emily Fowler LADY BETTY NOEL. Mr. Joseph Hatton's adaptation of his tender novel *Clytie* was given at the Olympic, as were Mr. Gilbert's *Princess, Ne'er-do-Weel* and *Gretchen*, *The Great Pink Pearl* and *The Pointsman* of Messrs. Carton and Raleigh, and the *Alone in London* of Mr. Robert Buchanan and Miss Harriet Jay. Recent experiments at this house have had little interest.

CHAPTER VI.

The share in the theatrical renascence of the two great patent houses, Covent Garden and Her Majesty's—until the reconstruction of the latter and its management by Mr. Tree—was the slightest conceivable. In the early days of the Victorian reign Covent Garden witnessed such performances of tragedy as mark the closing years of the Kemble period. Here in 1829, in order to rescue her father, who was over head and ears in debt, Fanny Kemble had been seen on the stage as JULIET; here four years later Edmund Kean ended his career; here four years later still Miss Helen Faucit made her London *début*. Macready followed with important Shakespearian revivals, retiring with heavy loss. Madame Vestris made a praiseworthy attempt to retrieve the fortunes of the house, and with her retirement, after the production, on 4th March, 1841, of Boucicault's *London Assurance*, the dramatic annals close. With *Babil and Bijou*, by Boucicault and Planché, the most ruinously costly production then, 1872, or probably since put on the stage, it reopened for a season. Miss Helen Barry in this was superbly statuesque as the PRINCESS.

Records during this century of Her Majesty's before April, 1897, when the new house was opened by Mr. Tree, are monopolised by opera and ballet. On the 19th November, 1866, Falconer took the theatre in order to produce his drama of *Oonagh*, which was so long that its performance was never finished. Among the fiascoes which the century witnessed, this was probably the most conspicuous.

The record of the Haymarket during the period of decline and that of renascence is perhaps the most honourable of any London theatre. Its history after the close of Genest's account of the stage, and previous to 1865, consists principally of the doings of Benjamin Webster and John Baldwin Buckstone, successive managers. Webster's direction began in 1837, thus synchronising with the accession of Her Majesty. Macready, Mrs. Warner, Mrs. Glover, Mrs. Nisbett, Strickland and Elton were his chief actors, and his early productions included *The Bridal*, a recasting of *The Maid's Tragedy*, by Beaumont and Fletcher, Sam Lover's *The White Horse of the Peppers*, and various pieces by Sheridan Knowles. Charles and Ellen Kean, Charles James Mathews and Madame Vestris, Anderson and Miss Helen Faucit were engaged, and plays by Boucicault, Robert Bell, Westland Marston, Douglas Jerrold, and other dramatists, succeeded each other. This was the period when Charles James Mathews reached the height of his popularity in impersonations such as SIR CHARLES COLDSTREAM in *Used Up*. Webster's offer in 1843 of £500 for the best comedy only produced Mrs. Gore's *Quid pro Quo*, which was a failure. Macready's farewell performances followed. American actors, the Wallacks and Hackett, and, much later, Edwin Booth, were seen. Barry Sullivan made his London *début* as HAMLET, and Mr. Toole, his first appearance on the stage, as SIMMONS in *The Spitalfields Weaver*. *Masks and Faces*, by Reade and Taylor, in which Webster played his great part of TRIPLET and Mrs. Stirling was PEG WOFFINGTON, was produced 20th November, 1852, and was the most conspicuous success of Webster's management, which concluded the following year.

THE STAGE IN THE YEAR 1900: A SOUVENIR.

Buckstone then opened the theatre characteristically enough with *The Rivals*, in which Mr. W. H. Chippendale "from America" made as SIR ANTHONY ABSOLUTE his first appearance. During Buckstone's management, revivals of old comedy, in which Buckstone, Compton — unequalled in Shakespearian clowns — Chippendale, Rogers, Mrs. Fitzwilliam, and many other well-known actors, took part, were a constant and pleasing feature, while farces by Maddison Morton and others constituted the most exhilarating of entertainments. At this time the audience was always played in at seven o'clock by a farce and played out about midnight by a second. In these farces Buckstone and Compton were unsurpassable in mirthfulness. Among successes with more serious pieces were *An Unequal Match*, in which Miss Amy Sedgwick appeared, and *The Overland Route*, with Charles James Mathews. In spite of all the efforts of the manager—who, like Triplet, was author, actor and manager in one — the theatre was drifting to ruin when Sothern, in *Our American Cousin*, arrested the ebbing tide. At first neither piece nor actor quite hit the public taste, and there was a good chance of both being withdrawn. Soon, however, LORD

DUNDREARY became the most popular character in London, and Sothern on the 22nd April, 1867, played the part for the 477th time.

Seeking, naturally, to work so profitable a mine, Sothern was seen in *Lord Dundreary Married and Done For*, *Brother Sam*, and other imitations or continuations. A good deal of extravagance and caricature distinguished these parts, but they were clever and exhilarating, and LORD DUNDREARY was at the outset a genuine creation.

In what was wrongly regarded as Miss Ellen Terry's *début* in *The Little Treasure*, Sothern was CAPTAIN MAYDENBLUSH to her GERTRUDE. As DAVID GARRICK in Robertson's adaptation of *Sullivan* he maintained his popularity, which he increased as FRANK ANERLY in Marston's *Favourite of Fortune*, as HARRY VIVIAN in Taylor's *Lessons for Life*, as the MARQUIS DE TOURVILLE in a *Hero of Romance* (*Le Roman d'un jeune homme pauvre*), and as COLONEL WHITE in *Home* (*L'Aventurière*). In these characters he showed himself an admirable comedian, though his pathos was forced, hard and ineffective. Supported by Buckstone, who was never responsible for an impersonation but was always delightfully quaint and mirthful, by Compton, Chippendale,

Mrs. Chippendale, Miss Madge Robertson (afterwards Mrs. Kendal), Miss Caroline Hill, and others, he bore the burden of the Haymarket. After visiting the United States he reappeared and played FITZ ALTAMONT in Byron's *Crushed Tragedian*, and other parts of no great importance. Performances that call for notice are *New Men and Old Acres*, by Tom Taylor and Mr. A. W. Dubourg, in which Miss Madge Robertson, the Chippendales, Howe, Buckstone and Mrs. Fitzwilliam distinguished themselves; Mr. Gilbert's *Palace of Truth*, in which Miss Robertson was ZEOLIDE; his *Pygmalion and Galatea*, in which she was GALATEA; his *Wicked World*, in which she was SELENE; and his *Charity*, in which she was MRS. VAN BRUGH. *Anne Boleyn*, played in February, 1875, introduced Miss Neilson as the heroine, and brought on the Haymarket stage Mr. Harold Kyrle, since known as Mr. Kyrle Bellew. Miss Neilson was also seen as JULIET, ROSALIND, ISABELLA in *Measure for Measure*, VIOLA and JULIA in *The Hunchback*. Mr. Hermann Vezin gave a fine presentation of the hero of Mr. Gilbert's *Dan'l Druce*, and Miss Marion Terry was enchanting as BELINDA TREHERNE in Mr. Gilbert's *Engaged*, in which

Mr. Kyrle Bellew, George Honey, Mr. F. Dewar and Miss Emily Thorne were also seen. After many experiments of doubtful value—the most interesting of which was Wills's *Ellen, or Love's Cunning*, afterwards called *Brag*, with Miss Florence Terry as the heroine and Mr. Charles Kelly in a character part, and some performances of " classic " comedy supported by Mrs. Bernard Beere as LYDIA LANGUISH and LADY TEAZLE, John S. Clarke, Howe and Terriss—Clarke retired from the management which had lapsed into his hands, and in which he was succeeded by Mr. and Mrs. Bancroft, who opened 31st January, 1880, with a revival of *Money*. On this occasion Mrs. Bancroft was LADY FRANKLIN, Miss Marion Terry CLARA DOUGLAS, Miss Linda Dietz GEORGINA VESEY, Mr. Bancroft SIR FREDERICK BLOUNT, Mr. Forbes-Robertson LORD GLOSSMORE, Mr. Archer DUDLEY SMOOTH, Arthur Cecil GRAVES, Mr. Conway ALFRED EVELYN, Mr. Henry Kemble STOUT, Mr. C. Brookfield SHARP, Mr. Odell SIR JOHN VESEY, and Mr. Vollaire the old MEMBER OF THE CLUB. Many revivals of Robertsonian comedy with well-chosen casts followed; and Mr. Clement Scott's delightful adaptation from Feuillet—*The*

Vicarage—was reproduced with an admirable cast consisting of the Bancrofts, Arthur Cecil, and Mr. Stewart-Dawson. *Masks and Faces*, with Mr. Bancroft as TRIPLET and Mrs. Bancroft as PEG WOFFINGTON, succeeded, and was followed by a revival of *Plot and Passion* and the production of *A Lesson*—Mr. Burnand's adaptation of *Lolotte*. For the performances of *Odette*, Mr. Clement Scott's adaptation from M. Sardou, Madame Modjeska was engaged and played the heroine. *Nearly Seven*, a bright monologue of Mr. Charles Brookfield, preceded a revival of *The Overland Route*, in which Mrs. John Wood, Mr. Alfred Bishop and Mr. David James took part. In Mr. Herman Merivale's version of *Fédora*, Mrs. Bernard Beere gave her remarkable performance of the heroine; Mrs. Bancroft was the COUNTESS OLGA, Mr. Coghlan LORIS IPANOFF, and Mr. Bancroft JEAN DE SIRIEX. Mr. Pinero's *Lords and Commons* added to the company Mrs. Stirling and Miss Calhoun, and brought back Messrs. Forbes-Robertson, Brookfield, and Elliot. In a revival of *The Rivals* Mr. Pinero was SIR ANTHONY, Mrs. Bernard Beere JULIA, Mrs. Stirling MRS. MALAPROP, Mr. Forbes-Robertson CAPTAIN ABSOLUTE, Miss Calhoun LYDIA LANGUISH, Mr. Bancroft FAULKLAND,

and Mr. Lionel Brough BOB ACRES. The piece was mounted with superfluous luxury, as has been the case in many subsequent revivals. Most of the pieces given during this occupancy of the Haymarket had been seen previously at the Prince of Wales's. *Diplomacy*, the authorship of which was avowed by Mr. Clement Scott and Mr. B. C. Stephenson, was given with Miss Calhoun in place of Mrs. Kendal as DORA, Mrs. Bernard Beere as COUNTESS ZICKA, Miss Le Thiere as the MARQUISE, and Mrs. Bancroft as LADY FAIRFAX. Mr. Barrymore supplanted as ORLOFF Mr. Bancroft, who took the part of the elder BEAUCLERC, the younger being played by Mr. Forbes-Robertson, who succeeded Mr. Kendal, Mr. C. Brookfield replaced Arthur Cecil as BARON STEIN, and Mr. Elliot was ALGIE. After holding the theatre for something less than six years the Bancrofts retired from management on the 20th July, 1885. *Dark Days*, by Mr. Hugh Conway and Mr. Comyns Carr, with Miss Lingard, Mr. Tree, Mr. R. Pateman, Mr. Sugden and Mr. Barrymore; *The Crisis*, adapted by James Albery; *Jim the Penman*, written by Sir Charles Young, in which Lady Monckton made her first appearance; and *Hard Hit*,

THE STAGE IN THE YEAR 1900: A SOUVENIR.

by Mr. Henry Arthur Jones, succeeded each other. Transferring his company from the Comedy, Mr. Tree began his management of the Haymarket. He had already attracted attention as SIR ANDREW AGUECHEEK, LAMBERT STREYKE in *The Colonel*, PRINCE BOROWSKI in Mr. Grundy's *Glass of Fashion*, PAOLO MACARI in *Called Back*, PHILIP DUNCKLEY in *Breaking a Butterfly* (Ibsen's *Doll's House*), the REV. ROBERT SPALDING in *The Private Secretary*, JOSEPH SURFACE, SIR MERVYN FERRAND in *Dark Days*, and BARON HARTFELD in *Jim the Penman*, and was regarded as foremost among the younger school of comedians. In *The Red Lamp*, produced 20th April, 1887, under his own management at the Comedy, and afterwards transferred to the Haymarket, he made a great stride as PAUL DEMETRIUS, the wily and sinister chief of police. *The Ballad Monger*, adapted by Messrs. Pollock and Besant from the *Gringoire* of M. Theodore de Banville, showed Mr. Tree's mastery of the poetic drama, which was further illustrated as BORGFELDT in *Partners*, Mr. Buchanan's adaptation of *Fromont jeune et Risler ainé*. *The Pompadour* of Wills and Mr. Grundy showed him as NARCISSE, and *Captain Swift* as WILDING, the bushranger, to the MRS. SEABROOK of Lady Monckton. Dismissing briefly MATTHEW RUDDOCK in Mr. H. A. Jones's *Wealth*, TRIPLET in *Masks and Faces*, and a dual part in Mr. Buchanan's *A Man's Shadow*, one may not so lightly overlook FALSTAFF, a marvellously thoughtful, intellectual and humorous performance, a VILLAGE PRIEST in Mr. Grundy's play so named—a species of French counterpart to the *Vicar of Wakefield*—and BEAU AUSTIN, a singularly striking piece of character-acting in the play of Mr. W. E. Henley and R. L. Stevenson. *The Dancing Girl* of Mr. Henry Arthur Jones, besides exhibiting an admirably striking impersonation by Mr. Tree of the Duke of Guiseburg, revealed the wonderful beauty and charm of Miss Julia Neilson as the heroine, in which she was temporarily succeeded by Miss Beatrice Lamb, whose promising *début* was made under Mr. Tree, and the tenderness of poor Miss Norreys as a lame girl. Mr. Tree's HAMLET is one of the four or five presentations of the part which rank among the highest interpretations of the modern stage. Mr. Stuart Ogilvie's *Hypatia*, a tragedy in resonant blank verse, revealed Miss Julia Neilson as a stately and poetical heroine, Mr. Tree as a striking and powerful ISSACHAR, Mr. Lewis Waller as a sinister ORESTES,

Mr. Fred Terry as PHILAMMON, and Miss Olga Brandon as RUTH. *A Woman of No Importance* of the late Oscar Wilde is remembered for the wit and sauciness of the dialogue, and for the bevy of women, all clever, and most of them fair, represented by Miss Julia Neilson, Mrs. Bernard Beere, Mrs. Tree, Miss Rose Leclercq, Miss Le Thiere, and others; and for fine performances by Mr. Tree and Mr. F. Terry. Ibsen's *Enemy of the People*, with Mr. Tree as STOCKMANN, was a bold experiment, though the piece was played for a few occasions only. Miss Hanbury was PETRA, Mr. Kemble was the burgomaster, Mr. Welch HOVSTAD, Mr. Allan Morten KILL. In spite of a picturesque presentation by Mr. Tree of the evil one, *The Tempter* of Mr. Henry Arthur Jones was little more remunerative than a *succès d'estime*. More can scarcely be advanced in favour of *The Charlatan* of Mr. Buchanan, the *Once Upon a Time* of Mr. Tree and Mr. Louis N. Parker, *A Modern Eve* by Mr. Malcolm Salaman, and *John-a-Dreams* by Mr. Haddon Chambers. *A Bunch of Violets*, however, a readaptation by Mr. Grundy of *Montjoye*—previously, in a different rendering from the same source, produced as *Mammon*—proved both stimulating and remunerative, thanks in a great measure to a fine piece of acting by Mrs. Tree as MRS. MURGATROYD. Mr. Tree's SIR PHILIP MARCHANT, Mr. Nutcombe Gould's VISCOUNT MOUNT SORRELL, Mr. Lionel Brough's MARK MURGATROYD, and Miss Lily Hanbury's LADY MARCHANT were noteworthy. *An Ideal Husband*, by Oscar Wilde, was played by Mr. and Mrs. Lewis Waller, Miss Julia Neilson, Miss Fanny Brough, Miss Vane Featherstone, Miss Maude Millett, Miss Helen Forsyth, and Messrs. Hawtrey, Brookfield, Lewis Waller and Cosmo Stuart, and was transferred to the Criterion. It was followed in the autumn by *Trilby*, Mr. Tree's last production at the Haymarket, and up to that time the most successful venture of his management. During many months *Trilby* was hailed as the greatest of modern triumphs. It made the fortune of that gentle soul Du Maurier—who, however, did not live long to enjoy his wealth—and brought to the theatre some of the largest receipts which in its long and varied experience it had known. Miss Dorothea Baird, the representative of the Thetis-like heroine, sprang at once into high reputation and has since remained one of the most prized of our younger actresses. Mr. Tree's SVENGALI, a being at once deadly and fantastic, is, in its line, unsurpassed among that actor's various creations. Miss Rosina Filippi, Mr. Edmund Maurice, Mr. Lionel Brough, Mr. Charles Allan, Mr. Gerald Du Maurier, Mr. H. V. Esmond and Mr. Holman Clark were among those who contributed to a "phenomenal" success.

Mrs. Tree, previously Miss Maud Holt, a brilliant amateur who had played at the St. James's LADY BETTY NOEL in *Lady Clancarty*, had yielded her husband fine support as PRINCESS CLAUDIA in *The Red Lamp*, STELLA DARBISHIRE in *Captain Swift*, DOROTHY MUSGRAVE in *Beau Austin*, LOYSE in *The Ballad Monger*, "Sweet" ANNE PAGE—in which she sang delightfully Mr. Swinburne's "Love laid his weary head"—and other parts. A result of the pecuniary receipts of *Trilby* was the transference by Mr. Tree of his management to the beautiful theatre erected on a portion of the site occupied by Her Majesty's, and the succession to the management of the Haymarket of Mr. Cyril Maude and Mr. Frederick Harrison.

Almost alone among actors, Mr. Maude had shown his capacity to play eccentric comedy (a range of parts of which the best exponent had been perhaps Colley Cibber, as seen in Grisoni's picture of that actor as LORD FOPPINGTON), including characters such as SIR BENJAMIN BACKBITE, TONY LUMPKIN, and BOB ACRES. Again and again at various theatres, and notably at the Comedy, Mr. Maude had revealed the range of his gifts and the value of a style which, though wanting perhaps in breadth, was admirable in delicacy. In his wife, Miss Winifred Emery, meanwhile he possessed an actress who, while belonging to the youngest school, had by inheritance, as well as by natural endowment, all the graces and distinction of the old. Under the management of Mr. Comyns Carr she had shown at the Comedy her marvellous art as ROSAMUND in Mr. Grundy's *Sowing the Wind*, and as THEOPHILA in Mr. Pinero's *Benefit of the Doubt*, and had, as MISS LINLEY, in Mr. Buchanan's *Dick Sheridan*, strengthened the notion, already formed from her performances in old comedy, that she was born to be a representative of the heroines of Goldsmith and Sheridan, as well as of those of Congreve and Farquhar, should ever these brilliant and shameless creatures be allowed to reappear on our stage.

We were in 1896 in the full tide of a romantic reaction. The new management of Mr. Maude and

THE STAGE IN THE YEAR 1900: A SOUVENIR.

Mr. Frederick Harrison began its career accordingly with *Under the Red Robe*, by Messrs. Stanley Weyman and Edward Rose, in which Miss Emery showed a few of her gifts, including her poetic fragrance as RENÉE DE COCHEFORÊT. Mr. Herbert Waring realised superbly the hero GIL DE BERAULT, Mr. Cyril Maude essayed a new line as CAPTAIN LAROLLE, and Mr. Sydney Valentine as RICHELIEU, Mr. Bernard Gould, Miss Eva Moore and Miss Fanny Coleman gave all possible picturesqueness and spirit to the French life of the seventeenth century. Still in the romantic revival was the management of the Haymarket when it produced Mr. Grundy's *Marriage of Convenience*, an adaptation of *Un Mariage sous Louis XV*. Miss Emery was once more irresistible as what Brantôme calls *une grande dame de par le monde*. Mr. Cyril Maude gave a picture of aristocratic eccentricity. Mr. William Terriss supplied a splendidly picturesque and gallant misreading of the COMTE DE CANDALE, and Miss Adrienne Dairolles, Mr. Valentine, Mr. Holman Clark, and other actors, made up a brilliant cast for a piece mounted to perfection.

With the *Little Minister* of Mr. J. M. Barrie—which, though it takes liberties with the original, which we should resent were they made by any other than the author, is a work of **true genius**—Mr. and Mrs. Maude got on the right tack. Though not quite ideal, the REV. GAVIN DISHART of the former was as good a conception as we are likely to see, while the LADY BABBIE of the latter is perhaps the most delightfully amorous, sparkling and mutinous creature the actress has presented. It is the highest homage to LADY BABBIE to say that she dwells in the memory with DIANA VERNON. Auld licht Elders and other Scottish folk were superbly presented by Mr. Brandon Thomas, Mr. Tyler, Mr. Kinghorne, Mr. Valentine, Mr. Holman Clark, Miss Sydney Fairbrother, and Mrs. E. H. Brooke.

Next came *The Manœuvres of Jane*, by Mr. Henry Arthur Jones, a play brimming with humour and character, but which begot a difference of opinion, not easily appeased, between author and management. Not before had Miss Emery played so spoilt, capricious and whimsical a heroine as JANE NANGLE. She contrived to imbue the character with a large measure of provocation and fascination. Miss Gertrude Kingston was a comfortably and ingenuously self-seeking young lady, and Miss Beatrice Ferrar was a "little horror." Mr. Cyril Maude was a meek and guileless nobleman, and Mr. Frederick Harrison, usually occupied with managerial cares, came forward to play his lordship's uncle. Mr. Esmond's drama, *Grierson's Way*, produced at an afternoon entertainment, does not belong to the Maude-Harrison management any more than *The Degenerates* of Mr. Grundy, given by Mrs. Langtry as a summer entertainment. *The Degenerates*, in which Mrs. Langtry was charged with playing the character of a certain well-known actress too much to the life, had the luck to shock the susceptibilities of the public on both sides of the Atlantic. Mrs. Langtry played the heroine, Miss Lily Grundy made a pleasing *début*, and Mr. Hawtrey, Mr. Gottschalk, Miss Lily Hanbury, and Miss Lottie Venne, attracted notice.

Returning to their own home, Messrs. Maude and Harrison produced *The Black Tulip*, Mr. Grundy's version of *La Tulipe Noire*, with Miss Emery as the heroine, the Jailer's daughter, Mr. Maude as the Dutch TULIPOMANIAC, and Mr. Harrison as WILLIAM OF ORANGE. After this had run a successful career, the management turned to classical comedy, and gave us in turn *She Stoops to Conquer*, *The Rivals*, and *The School for Scandal*, as well mounted and played as they often have been at the house which is their recognised home. Miss

Emery has been in every case the heroine, establishing thus the highest position in comedy, and Mr. Maude has given effective and humorous presentations of comic characters. These representations, which exhibit the stage at its best in one all-important line, are fresh in the public memory, and *The School for Scandal*, after a season with Miss Julia Neilson as NELL GWYNN and Mr. F. Terry as CHARLES II, came back to the Haymarket.*

<small>* The latest success has been scored with *Second in Command*, by Captain Robert Marshall; the heroine of which, in the enforced absence of Miss Emery, is presented by Miss Sibyl Carlisle.</small>

Transferring himself to Her Majesty's, Mr. Tree began his occupancy none too well with the production, on the 28th April, 1897, of Mr. Gilbert Parker's *Seats of the Mighty*. Though dramatic in conception and heroic in strain, the play had few elements of popularity. Mr. Tree assigned to TINOIR DOLTAIRE a philosophical, meditative villainy which, though lacking in sympathy, was in its way effective. Mrs. Tree showed her fine talents to advantage as MADAME COURNAL. She also delivered with much charm a rhymed address by the Laureate. Mr. Brookfield was LOUIS XV, Mr. Lewis Waller CAPTAIN MORAY, Mr. Murray Carson FRANÇOIS BIGOT, Miss Janette Steer the POMPADOUR, and Miss Kate Rorke ALICE DUVARNEY. After some revivals of former triumphs Mr. Tree produced *The*

Silver Key, Mr. Grundy's version of *Mademoiselle de Belle-Isle*, in which he was a brilliant DUC DE RICHELIEU, Miss Evelyn Millard was MADEMOISELLE DE BELLE-ISLE, Mrs. Tree a fine MARQUISE DE PRIE, and Mr. Lewis Waller the CHEVALIER D'AUBIGNY.

With a noble revival of *Julius Cæsar*, Mr. Tree, on 22nd January, 1898, began the great series of Shakespearian revivals which have been the chief distinction of his management. The mounting of this was the best that has been seen, and the performance eclipsed the memories of the Saxe-Meiningen presentation of the same play.

The MARK ANTONY of Mr. Tree, the CÆSAR of Mr. Fulton, Mr. Lewis Waller's BRUTUS, the late Mr. McLeay's CASSIUS, Mr. Louis Calvert's CASCA, Mrs. Tree's LUCIUS, Miss Lily Hanbury's CALPHURNIA and Miss Evelyn Millard's PORTIA are vividly remembered. The designs of Sir Alma Tadema, R.A., were worthy of that best depictor of Roman beauty and art. This historic tragedy has since been revived with a cast widely different from that it first received. *Ragged Robin*, Mr. Louis N. Parker's adaptation of *Le Chemineau* of M. Jean Richepin, opened out a new line. No piece idealising like this the life of a tramp—in England not a popular and scarcely a presentable character—had been seen. In Mr. Tree's *Ragged Robin* we recognised that the roads had a beauty like the woods, and an appeal like the sea, and the full poetry of a character with something of the tenderness of a Gringoire was realised. A fragrant performance of ALISON was given by Mrs. Tree, and Miss Evelyn Millard's NANCY, Mr. Warner's powerful JAN PERROTT, Mr. McLeay's FARMER STOKES, and Mr. Lewis Waller's MANLY JACK were excellent. Waving fields of golden corn and orchards of russet apples gave a sweet suggestion of fecundity.

After lending the theatre for a couple of months to Miss Olga Nethersole—who produced *The Termagant* of Messrs. Louis N. Parker and Murray Carson, in which she played the heroine, supported by Mr. Barnes, Mr. Abingdon, Mr. Paulton, Miss Esmé Beringer, Miss Eva Williams and Miss Grace Warner—Mr. Tree opened the season 1898-1899 with *The Musketeers*, Mr. Sydney Grundy's adaptation of *Les Trois Mousquetaires* of Dumas. Another version of the same original with Mrs. Lewis Waller as MILADI, written by Mr. Henry Hamilton, and produced the previous year at the Métropole, Camberwell, had been revived on the 2nd October

THE STAGE IN THE YEAR 1900: A SOUVENIR.

at the Globe, and has since once more been given at the Lyceum. Opinion was divided as to the merit of the respective adaptations. That at Her Majesty's was, at least, the more gorgeous as a spectacle. The principal features in a powerful cast were Mrs. Tree as ANNE OF AUSTRIA, Mrs. Brown-Potter as MILADI, a part for which this actress seemed born, Miss Mabel Love as CONSTANCE, Mr. Tree as D'ARTAGNAN, Mr. Lewis Waller as BUCKINGHAM, Mr. McLeay as RICHELIEU, Mr. Charles Allan as BONACIEUX, Mr. H. Ross as LOUIS XIII, and Messrs. Mills, Louis Calvert, and Du Maurier as ATHOS, PORTHOS, and ARAMIS.

The next novelty—12th April, 1899—was Mr. Henry Arthur Jones's *Carnac Sahib*, a study of Anglo-Indian loves and animosities, which deserved a warmer reception than it obtained. Its pictures of the proceedings of English matrons were free and animated; a marvellous presentation of existence in India was furnished, and many of the performers were as lifelike as they could be. Mrs. Brown-Potter as OLIVE ARNISON had a fatal and snake-like allurement, the quarrels of the two Colonels—once friends—were highly realistic and impressive in the hands of Mr. Tree and Mr. Waller, and performances of Mr.

Beveridge, Miss Eva Moore, and others, won high recognition. The ways of the makers and holders of India were never better shown on the stage. *King John*, produced for the opening of the season 1899-1900, constitutes another of Mr. Tree's Shakespearian triumphs. Miss Julia Neilson essayed a dangerous experiment as CONSTANCE, and was rewarded by a success proportionate to the risks she ran, establishing herself as the best exponent of the part to be recalled. Mr. Tree's KING JOHN was marvellous in intensity and variety, the death scene being most impressive. Mr. Lewis Waller was the BASTARD, Mr. McLeay HUBERT, Mr. Mollison PHILIP OF FRANCE, Mr. Gerald Lawrence LEWIS, Mr. Calvert the CARDINAL, and Miss Bateman QUEEN ELINOR. The scenery and dresses constituted an historical revelation.

The performance at the Haymarket of the first part of *King Henry IV* belongs to an earlier date, but as one of Mr. Tree's best Shakespearian productions should not be dismissed without mention. It had been produced on the afternoon of the 8th May, 1896, and exhibited Mr. Tree in his wonderful make-up as FALSTAFF, Mr. Lewis Waller as HOTSPUR, and Miss Kate Phillips as DAME QUICKLY.

THE STAGE IN THE YEAR 1900: A SOUVENIR.

To the 10th of January of the present year belongs the most poetical presentation of *A Midsummer Night's Dream* that the stage has seen, with Mr. Tree as the most philosophical of BOTTOMS, Mrs. Tree as the daintiest of TITANIAS, and Miss Julia Neilson as the loveliest and most imperial of OBERONS, and with a *mise en scène* that was ravishing. The same year saw a presentation of *Rip van Winkle* that suffered somewhat from the moral rehabilitation of the character of the hero. The house reopened in September, 1900, with a revival of *Julius Cæsar*, in which Mr. Robert Taber was an admirable CASSIUS, in the place of Mr. McLeay, whose premature death was an appreciable loss to the stage. Mr. Stephen Phillips's *Herod*, a greatly conceived work, was given on the last day of October, and still holds possession of the stage.

CHAPTER VII.

THE influence, not only upon the houses which came into existence after the revival of interest in the theatres, but also upon those long existing homes of the drama, the managements of which had the sense to realise the new requirements of the stage, to set their sails to the trade wind which had sprung up and to profit by forces they themselves had not set in motion, has been closely followed, and it has been shown how steadfast and continuous has been the progress from a period of unprecedented decay to one of triumph equally unprecedented. The lesson insisted upon at the outset has been enforced, and the right of the English stage to stand erect by the side of that of any other nation has been established. Other houses which, though they escaped the heat and toil of the day, have shared in the spoils of victory, are entitled to a measure of recognition.

THE STAGE IN THE YEAR 1900: A SOUVENIR.

On its first opening, 21st March, 1874, the Criterion inspired some interest as the first underground theatre, but gave little promise of the distinction to which it was to attain. Performances began under the management of Byron and Kingston with *The American Lady* of the former—in which, after his occasional wont, Byron played a principal part—and a musical extravaganza by Mr. W. S. Gilbert. David Fisher, John Clarke, Mrs. John Wood and Mr. Barnes were numbered among the company. The theatre took no strong hold on the public until 3rd April, 1877, when Mr. Charles Wyndham made, in Albery's adaptation *Pink Dominoes*, his first great success at a house the mainstay and manager of which he was to become. Associated with him were Mr. Herbert Standing, Mr. Ashley, Augustus Harris, Miss Eastlake, Miss Fanny Josephs, Miss Edith Bruce, and Mdlle. Camille Clermont. Severely censured for immorality, *Pink Dominoes* taught the public the way to the theatre which was soon afterwards to establish itself as an English Palais Royal, in no way inferior to its model. Mr. Bronson Howard's *Truth* was among the pieces then seen, and Mr. Burnand's *Betsy*, given on the 6th August, 1879, had a success rivalling that of *Pink Dominoes*. *Where's the Cat?* by Albery, 20th November, 1880, had a very strong cast, comprising Messrs. Wyndham, Standing, Giddens, W. J. Hill, Mrs. John Wood, Misses Rose Saker, Mary Rorke, Edith Bruce and Eastlake. Mr. Gilbert's *Foggerty's Fairy* was produced on the 15th December, 1881, and Albery's *Featherbrain* on the 23rd June, 1884, while *The Candidate*, adapted by Mr. J. H. McCarthy from *Le Député de Bombignac*, brought to an end what may not be the most important, but was certainly the most amusing, period in Criterion annals. At no London theatre had light comedy so artistic and so exhilarating been exhibited. Mr. Wyndham had been the life of all, but his associates did yeoman service. With Mr. Wyndham's assumption of management more ambitious and no less successful experiments came into fashion. At the time, 1885, when Mr. Wyndham took the management of the Criterion—at which house, after a little vacillation, he settled down into a steady stride of success—he had become inspired, like Cleopatra, with "immortal longings." At this time, too, he became associated with Miss Mary Moore, during subsequent years his close and constant ally and the sharer in his every triumph, including his performances in Germany and Russia, when by Imperial command he proceeded from Leipsic to St. Petersburg. With her aid, he began, with *Wild Oats*, a long and prosperous career in comedy. *Wild Oats* had scarcely been seen, if seen at all, since Miss Henrietta Hodson had appeared as the demurest of LADY AMARANTHS at the Royalty. Miss Moore was the meekest and most alluring of Quaker heroines, and Mr. Wyndham, as ROVER, showed his capacity to replace Mathews in these light comedy parts of which he long had had a monopoly. As DAVID GARRICK, created by Sothern, Mr. Wyndham established himself permanently in favour, and the *rôle* was held yesterday, as it is to-day, the first in his repertory. In like fashion Miss Moore has been accepted and is still cherished as the ideal ADA INGOT. After these beginnings, Mr. Wyndham gave the world at the Criterion a series of performances constituting what may be called his second method. In a revival of *She Stoops to Conquer*, with Mr. Giddens as TONY LUMPKIN, Mr. S. Valentine as DIGGORY, and Mr. Blakeley and Miss M. A. Victor as MR. and MRS. HARDCASTLE, he played

YOUNG MARLOW in brightest style to the delightful MISS HARDCASTLE of Miss Moore. *Still Waters Run Deep* was revived, and showed Mr. Wyndham and Miss Moore as JOHN MILDMAY and MRS. MILDMAY, Mrs. Bernard Beere as Mrs. STERNHOLD, and Miss Ellaline Terriss as EDITH CLINTON. A revival of *London Assurance* followed, with Miss Moore as GRACE HARKAWAY, Mrs. Bernard Beere as LADY GAY, Mr. Farren as SIR HARCOURT COURTLEY, Mr. Wyndham as DAZZLE, Mr. Bourchier as CHARLES, Mr. Giddens as DOLLY SPANKER, and Mr. Cyril Maude as COOL.

In *The School for Scandal* Mr. Wyndham was CHARLES SURFACE and Mr. Bourchier JOSEPH. Mrs. Bernard Beere was LADY TEAZLE, and Miss Moore MARIA. Messrs. Farren, Blakeley, Maude, Playfair, and Giddens were in the cast. Revivals of *Brighton* and *Pink Dominoes* followed.

Mention should also be made of the delightful duologue *Mrs. Hilary Regrets*. With *The Bauble Shop* of Mr. Henry Arthur Jones, Mr. Wyndham produced on the 26th January, 1893, the first of his serious and important novelties. In that work of fine contrasts the actor was seen at his best, as the all but "lost leader." Mr. Valentine gave

THE STAGE IN THE YEAR 1900: A SOUVENIR.

a picture of Radical vulgarity, and Miss Mary Moore, Miss Louise Moodie, Miss Ellis Jeffreys, Mr. Somerset (recalling his success in *Little Lord Fauntleroy*) and Mr. Allan Aynesworth established the triumph of a noteworthy work. *An Aristocratic Alliance*—an Anglification of *Le Gendre de M. Poirier*—brought together Mr. Wyndham, Mr. Groves, Mr. J. G. Taylor, and Mr. de Lange, uniting them with Miss Moore, Miss Fowler and Miss Annie Hughes. With *The Case of Rebellious Susan* of Mr. Jones, first seen 3rd October 1894, both actor and author reached their highest water-mark. For many months subsequent to its production London Society flocked to see its own features depicted by one of the sauciest and most daring of satirists. Outcry on ethical ground was provoked, and the question as to the extent of the vengeance of LADY SUSAN was contested. The heroine, as played by Miss Moore, was hugged to the heart of Society, Mr. Wyndham's SIR RICHARD KATO was treated as a masterpiece, and the characters generally, as played by Miss Gertrude Kingston, Miss Fanny Coleman, Miss Nina Boucicault, Mr. F. Kerr, Mr. C. P. Little, Mr. H. Kemble, and Mr. B. Webster, won universal admiration.

Mr. R. C. Carton made, on the 17th May, 1895, his appearance on boards he was profitably to occupy. *The Home Secretary*—with its quaint and romantic mixture of anarchism and romance, interpreted by Mr. Wyndham as the hero, Miss Julia Neilson as his wife, Miss Mary Moore as MRS. THORPE DIDSBURY, and Miss Maude Millett, Messrs. Brookfield, Sydney Brough, Bishop and Lewis Waller—acquired a popularity due to the wit of the dialogue and the merit of the presentation as much as to the strength or vraisemblance of the story. The basis of *The Squire of Dames*, also by Mr. Carton, which followed, was found in *L'Ami des Femmes* of Dumas fils. Though highly popular, the piece was not in its author's best line. It served, however, to bring on the English stage Miss Fay Davis, an American artist whose progress to the front has been Atalanta-like in rapidity. *Rosemary*, by Messrs. Louis N. Parker and Murray Carson, gave a refreshingly fragrant picture of early Victorian life, and told pensively and prettily a story of love and self-abnegation. The play gained greatly from its environment. Whether the last act is a source of strength or weakness is not easily determined. Miss Moore was, however, radiant as a Dickens-like heroine, Mr. Wyndham's SIR JASPER was a picture worthy of Leech, Mr. Alfred Bishop and Miss Carlotta Addison were a precious old couple, Mr. James Welch was a wonderful postillion, and Miss Annie Hughes as a domestic and Mr. Barnes as a philosopher and scholar were excellent.

Mr. Jones came again to the fore in 1897 with *The Physician*, and followed it up with *The Liars*. The former is a serious, earnest and psychological play, the central figure in which is a dipsomaniac advocate of temperance carefully elaborated by Mr. Thalberg. Mr. Wyndham himself appeared as a beneficent and agnostic doctor, and added to his fine company Miss Marion Terry, who was delightful as a society siren. In *The Liars* Mr. Jones went beyond the point he reached in *The Case of Rebellious Susan*. It is one of the wittiest, sprightliest, most diverting, and on the whole best acted comedies of its day. Everything in it dwells in the memory—the delicate, extravagant dinner at Shepperford, the frivolous and inconsequential explanations of LADY JESSICA, the quarrel between DERING and FALKNER, the man of the world and the visionary, and, most of all, the family council of liars, one of the most humorous and truly comic scenes ever depicted. It is difficult to praise highly enough each separate performer, but Mr. Wyndham's admirably reasonable, polished, sage and earnest Sir Christopher, Mr. Thalberg's passionate Falkner, Mr. Standing's morose and churlish Gilbert Nepean, and Mr. Bishop's meek and edifying Coke deserve mention. As Freddie Tatton Mr. Vane Tempest built up a reputation almost, it might be said, in a single performance. A bouquet of beauty and talent was supplied by Miss Moore, Miss Irene Vanbrugh, Miss Cynthia Brooke, Miss Sarah Brooke and Miss Janette Steer. In a strangely different line was *The Jest* of Messrs. Parker and Carson, in which Mr. Wyndham essayed, with a measure of success, a part romantic in conception and tragic in development. In this he was supported by Mr. Kyrle Bellew and Miss Cynthia Brooke, as well as Miss Moore. One more appearance was made by Mr. Wyndham before quitting the house he had raised to be one of the most popular of shrines. This consisted in playing Mr. Parbury, the victim of Mr. Haddon Chambers's humorous if rather misogynistic comedy, *The Tyranny of Tears*. On the 16th November, 1899, with a performance of *David Garrick*—the entire proceeds of which were given to the fund for the soldiers' wives and families—Mr. Wyndham opened the theatre which bears his name. Contenting himself with revivals, including one of Mr. Pinero's—*Dandy Dick*—he did not until the 19th April of the following year produce the adaptation by Messrs. Stuart Ogilvie and Louis N. Parker of *Cyrano de Bergerac*. His performance of this vapouring, insolent and self-denying hero divides public admiration with that of M. Coquelin, and is indeed, while not less picturesque, more humorous and less of a caricature than that of the creator of the part. The ROXANE of Miss Moore, the LISE of Miss Alice de Winton and the RAGUENEAU of Mr. Giddens were noteworthy features in a cast the longest probably that has ever been assigned an English play. For his winter experiment Mr. Wyndham produced in October, 1900, *Mrs. Dane's Defence*, Mr. Jones's masterpiece. This, admirably interpreted by Mr. Wyndham, Miss Lena Ashwell and Miss Moore, is the most popular piece at present occupying the stage.

Deserted practically by Mr. Wyndham, who, though retaining a share in the management, had transferred his services elsewhere, the Criterion stumbled on the best of fortune by producing the

Lady Huntworth's Experiment of Mr. R. C. Carton, a piece which all but alone among dramas of the year lasted through an entire summer and autumn management. Miss Compton (Mrs. Carton), always well suited by her husband, played with her usual breadth and stolidity as LADY HUNTWORTH, a countess masquerading as a cook; and Mr. Arthur Bourchier, Mr. Eric Lewis, Mr. Dion Boucicault, Mr. Ernest Hendrie and Miss Gertrude Elliott secured for the whole an artistic and comic interpretation. *A Noble Lord*, a bright but rather thin work of Captain Marshall, is the latest novelty at this house.

A mere mention suffices of the Aquarium theatre, subsequently called the Imperial, which was opened in 1876 or 1877 and to most intents and purposes closed in 1885, though it is to be shortly re-opened by Mrs. Langtry. While under the management of Miss Marie Litton it gave some eminently satisfactory revivals of old comedy. Frank Marshall's three-act comedy, *Family Honour*, was seen there 18th May, 1878; and Mr. Herman Merivale's *Lord of the Manor* 3rd January, 1880; and Mr. Buchanan's *Lucy Brandon* 8th April, 1882. In the revivals the chief interest was found. Among those who participated in them were Miss Litton herself, who in spite of, perhaps because of, a rather hard voice was admirable in fine ladies of old comedy, and constantly played the heroines, Mr. W. Farren, Mr. Ryder, Mr. Lionel Brough, Mrs. Stirling, Mr. Vezin, Mr. Kyrle Bellew, Mr. Forbes-Robertson, and occasionally Mr. Phelps and the best actors of these days. A revival of *As You Like It* at this house is remembered as one of the most unpretendingly poetical that has been given. Miss Litton's MISS HARDCASTLE was a gracious realisation of the character. Among other revivals were those of *The Beaux' Stratagem*—in which Miss Litton played Mrs. Oldfield's part of MRS. SULLEN—and Foote's *The Liar*. At this house Mrs. Langtry was first seen as ROSALIND.

CHAPTER VIII.

On the 10th of October, 1881, under the management of Mr. D'Oyly Carte, the Savoy theatre opened its doors with *Patience*, an opera of Mr. W. S. Gilbert transferred to this house from the Opéra Comique. Although the Lyceum theatre had borne for a time the title of the English Opera House; and the theatre from which *Patience* was transferred was called the Opéra Comique, no genuine home of English opera existed until the opening of the Savoy. An experiment in this direction had been made at Covent Garden, which had witnessed the first production of operas by Balfe, Wallace, Macfarren, and other English musicians. Nothing had come of this. The augmenting popularity of the pieces due to the Gilbert-Sullivan combination, inadequately produced at the Strand, the Opéra Comique, and elsewhere, called for a regular home for the most original,

THE STAGE IN THE YEAR 1900: A SOUVENIR.

vivacious and musical form of comic opera the English stage had seen. This the Savoy provided. As such, the house scarcely comes within the ken of this book. Many English actors who have achieved success in other careers won, however, their spurs at the Savoy; and some brief reference to the series of Gilbert-Sullivan operas there produced and their principal exponents becomes expedient.

Iolanthe, the first novelty given at this house, 25th November, 1882, worthily opened the series. A charming caprice, it was no less charmingly set forth; and with Mr. George Grossmith as the LORD CHANCELLOR, Miss Alice Barnett as the FAIRY QUEEN, Miss Jessie Bond as IOLANTHE, Mr. Rutland Barrington as the EARL OF MOUNT ARARAT, Mr. Durward Lely, Mr. Richard Temple, Misses Fortescue, Julia Gwynne, Sibyl Grey and Leonora Braham, it introduced most of those by whom the popularity of the house was won and its fortunes were established. The principal among the actors named supported *Princess Ida*, an opera founded upon Tennyson's *Princess*, and they appeared again in *The Mikado*, a piece in which a new line was happily struck out. The play last named is one of the most original, the most melodious, and the most characteristic works due to the combination. Mr. Grossmith's KO-KO attained the height of popularity, as did the POOH BAH of Mr. Barrington, the YUM YUM of Miss Braham, Miss Jessie Bond's PITTI SING, and Miss Rosina Brandram's KATISHA. *Ruddygore*, or *Ruddigore*, followed in 1886, while *The Yeomen of the Guard* the following year added to the company, among other recruits, Miss Geraldine Ulmar, Mr. Wallace Brownlow, Mr. Courtice Pounds and Mr. Denny. *The Gondoliers* introduced Mr. Frank Wyatt and Miss Decima Moore. In 1891 Mr. George Dance and Mr. Edward Solomon were responsible for *The Nautch Girl*; and in 1892, in a comic opera with romantic and sentimental music entitled *Haddon Hall*, Sir Arthur Sullivan had the practised co-operation of Mr. Sydney Grundy. The collaboration of Mr. Gilbert and Sir Arthur, abandoned as it seemed, was renewed, and on the 7th October, 1893, with a cast including, in addition to former favourites, Miss Nance M'Intosh, Miss E. Owen, Miss F. Perry and Mr. John Le Hay, *Utopia, Limited*, was given, which was far from the best result of the combination. Mr. Burnand was associated with

THE STAGE IN THE YEAR 1900: A SOUVENIR.

Sir Arthur in *The Chieftain*, an elaboration of *The Contrabandista*, and on the 7th March, 1896, another Gilbert and Sullivan opera was presented as *The Grand Duke*. Sir Arthur has since collaborated with Mr. Pinero and Mr. Comyns Carr in *The Beauty Stone*, and with Captain Basil Hood in *The Rose of Persia*, while Sir A. C. Mackenzie, Mr. Burnand and Mr. Lehmann were connected with *His Majesty*, but the association the theatre was designed to exploit has of late been known only through revivals.

To the same year as the Savoy belongs the Comedy, a house misnamed as regards its early experience, which belonged wholly to comic opera, generally of foreign growth. It witnessed the *Agnes* of Mr. Buchanan; the *Sister Mary* of Mr. Wilson Barrett and Mr. Clement Scott; the first production of *The Red Lamp* of Mr. Outram Tristram; *The Barrister*, a farcical comedy of Messrs. Manville Fenn and J. H. Darnley; *The Arabian Nights* of Mr. Grundy, transferred from the Globe; and Mr. Jerome's *Sisters*, and his delicate *Wood-Barrow Farm*. It did not, however, fairly justify its title or claim very serious consideration until it came into the hands of Mr. Comyns Carr, whose first piece there was his own *Nerves*, which was on the 9th June,

The death of Sir Arthur Sullivan while these pages are passing through the press is something like a national calamity.

(117)

1890, brilliantly interpreted by Mr. C. H. Hawtrey, Mr. Kemble, Mr. Righton, Mr. Wyes, Miss Maude Millett, Miss Lydia Cowell, and Miss Lottie Venne. *May and December*, adapted from Meilhac and Halévy by Mr. Grundy and Mr. Mackay, was transferred to the Comedy on the 13th November, and played by Messrs. Brookfield, Hawtrey, Graham and Wyes, and Misses Norreys, Cowell, and Ethel Mathews. It had, eight years previously, under the title *The Novel Reader*, been given at a private performance at the Globe, its public representation having been prohibited by the Censor. It had also been seen at the Criterion, where Mr. Gilbert Farquhar, as the benevolent and self-denying old book-worm, and Miss Kate Rorke, as the heroine, assigned the respective characters a setting of genuine comedy which enhanced the effect. Mr. Brookfield dramatised *Divorçons*, and produced it under the title of *To-day*, satirising in it the æsthetic craze and epicene exhibitions of Society. Mr. Brookfield, Mr. Hawtrey, Miss Lottie Venne and Miss Vane Featherstone took part in the performance.

With Mr. Grundy's *Sowing the Wind*, which may perhaps be reckoned its author's masterpiece, Mr. Comyns Carr's intellectual management established itself in public favour. A comedy striking a deep note of public sympathy, it was admirably supported by Mr. Brandon Thomas, who therein first revealed the extent of his histrionic power; Miss Winifred Emery as an earnest and womanly heroine, Mr. Sydney Brough as a bright young lover, Mr. Maude, Mr. Ian Robertson, Mr. Maurice, Mr. Dennis, Miss Rose Leclercq, and Miss Annie Hughes. To Mr. Buchanan's *Dick Sheridan* reference has been made elsewhere. In *The New Woman* Mr. Grundy maintained the high level he had reached in *Sowing the Wind*, displaying a still larger capacity, both emotional and literary, and betraying a more distinctly satirical purpose. Miss Emery and Mr. Cyril Maude, with Mr. Fred Terry, were seen once more to high advantage. During the summer of this year (1894) Mr. Willard had brought before us Mr. Barrie's delicate, pretty and fantastic idyl, *The Professor's Love Story*, and had won all hearts as the simple-minded PROFESSOR. Miss Bessie Hatton had assigned great tenderness and charm, not unmixed with shrewdness, to the heroine, and Mr. Royce Carleton and Mr. Tyler had delighted the playgoers with sketches of bucolic character. *The Prude's Progress* of Mr. Jerome and Mr. Phillpott, though produced at the Comedy, was soon transferred to Terry's, and the autumn season opened with Mr. Pinero's *Benefit of the Doubt*.

This admirable play indicates the high watermark of Mr. Pinero's purely comic achievement. A play with finer touches of satire and a more exquisite flavour, and one that reveals with more picturesque fidelity what is most fascinating and reprehensible in modern English society, cannot easily be indicated. If it comes short of enduring greatness it will be because the problem it presents is such a marvel of ingenuity that it defies solution. One must accept it as one of the questions in life to which no answer is possible, and there are in real life many such. If we were to select the two works which before all others prove that our stage as regards comedy may hold its head up beside the Comédie-Française and the Gymnase-Dramatique, we should point to *The Benefit of the Doubt* and *The Liars*. It may be doubted if either play has, during the present century, been surpassed. If a satisfactory issue for *The Benefit of the Doubt* could be provided, the work would be the best English comedy of modern times. It is not certain that even as it stands it is not entitled to that position. THEOPHILA FRASER, in the hands of Miss Winifred Emery, is a masterpiece, and the general cast, with Misses Rose Leclercq, Lily Hanbury, Eva Williams, and Esmé Beringer, and Messrs. Cyril Maude, Leonard Boyne, Graham and Pigott, would have done credit to any theatre in the two hemispheres.

Since the close of Mr. Carr's management many experiments of a less ambitious nature have been essayed, Mr. Charles Hawtrey inaugurating a reign of mirth, over which he presided until he ultimately transferred his throne to the Avenue. At the Comedy he gave on the 10th March, 1897, Mr. Burnand's *Saucy Sally*, which was followed by Mr. Esmond's pretty and happily named *One Summer's Day*, in which Miss Eva Moore merited golden opinions as MAYSIE, and by *Lord and Lady Algy*, perhaps Mr. Carton's masterpiece. In no part has the quiet, pathetic plausibility of Mr. Hawtrey's style been seen to greater advantage than in LORD ALGY, while in LADY ALGY Miss Compton's unsurpassable *aplomb* once more revealed itself. Mr. H. Kemble and Mr. Eric Lewis contributed to the spirit of the whole. The Comedy was also one of the homes of *Secret Service*, and witnessed the appearance of Miss Eleanor Calhoun, Miss May Palfrey and Mr. Gerald Lawrence in *A Lady of Quality*, an adaptation of Mrs. Burnett's dramatic novel so named. The house was then occupied by Miss Janette Steer, who appeared in Mr. Gilbert's *Pygmalion and Galatea* and *Comedy and Tragedy*. It is now in the hands of a German company. The same year that witnessed the opening of the Comedy saw also that of the Novelty, a house that, through its many transformations and changes of name, never "deviated" into success until in these later days it served for the revival by Mr. Penley of *A Little Ray of Sunshine* and *The Private Secretary*, and accepted the name of the Great Queen Street theatre.

CHAPTER IX.

Suspending for a while mention of the rapidly augmenting list of new houses, one turns to the St. James's, a theatre which, under Mr. Alexander's management, stands in the foremost rank. Built by John Braham, the singer—whose "folly" it was, and who invested in it all his savings—it opened in 1835 with a burletta by Mrs. Gilbert à Becket, in which Braham and Miss Priscilla Horton (Mrs. German Reed) took part. Situated in a portion of the West End unknown to the country visitor, it had an almost unique experience of calamity, a constant series of French plays by Rachel and other distinguished artists constituting its chief claim on attention. It had a monopoly of the plays of Dickens. Here in 1836 was produced *The Strange Gentleman*, with Harley as the principal, and *The Village Coquettes*, and in 1837 his *Is She His Wife?* Mrs. Stirling, Mrs. Honey,

Wright, Dowton, Wrench, Mrs. Glover, Frank Matthews and Alfred Wigan were among the exponents of these pieces. The spell was unbroken. Mitchell essayed French and German plays with moderate success, and Mrs. Seymour, Alfred Wigan, George Vining and Ben Webster tried their hands in management. *The Isle of St. Tropez* and *Lady Audley's Secret*, by George Roberts (Mr. Robert Walters), were among the few remunerative productions. The management of Miss Louisa Herbert was the best the theatre had then known. Miss Herbert herself, a woman of remarkable beauty and genuine talent, played agreeably and with distinction the heroines of old comedy. Under her, Irving and John Clayton appeared, the former as DORICOURT. Mrs. John Wood succeeded to the management, under which adaptations of *Le Dégel*, of *Frou-frou*, of *Fernande*, were seen. Robertson's *War* and Mr. Gilbert's *Tom Cobb* were produced, and some pretty dialogues of Theyre Smith inspired a faint interest. *Les Danischeffs* of M. Pierre Newski and the younger Dumas, adapted by Lord Newry (the Earl of Kilmorey), was a very powerful play, and obtained plenary recognition. Brilliantly acted by John

Clayton, Mr. Hermann Vezin, Mr. Charles Warner, Mrs. Wood, Miss Lydia Foote, and Miss Fanny Addison, it established for a while the fortunes of the house.

In 1879, with *Monsieur le Duc*, by Mr. Valentine Prinsep, R.A., and a revival of *The Queen's Shilling*, the St. James's opened under the management of Messrs. Hare and Kendal, taking a place it was permanently to occupy as one of the leading and most artistic theatres in London. In the former piece Mr. Hare was the DUC DE RICHELIEU; in the latter he was once more COLONEL DAUNT, Mrs. Kendal being KATE GREVILLE, and Mr. Kendal FRANK MAITLAND. The company included William Terriss, Mr. Wenman, Mr. Cathcart, Miss Kate Phillips, and Mrs. Gaston Murray. *The Falcon* of Lord Tennyson, with Mr. Kendal as the COUNT and Mrs. Kendal the LADY GIOVANNA, was one of the earliest productions, and was followed by Mr. Theyre Smith's *Old Cronies*, finely rendered by Mr. Mackintosh and Mr. Wenman. A revival of *Still Waters Run Deep* and a performance of *William and Susan* — an alteration by Wills of Jerrold's great naval play—followed, the latter with

Mrs. Kendal as SUSAN, Mr. Kendal as WILLIAM (one of his finest parts), Mr. Hare as the ADMIRAL, and Mr. Barnes as CAPTAIN CROSSTREE.

The Squire by Mr. Pinero, produced on the 29th December, 1881, was the first genuinely important novelty of the new management. It is a sweetly bucolic piece, in which, as KATE VERITY, otherwise the SQUIRE, Mrs. Kendal was harrowing. *The Money Spinner* of the same brilliant author was handicapped by being in two acts; a third was subsequently added. The MILLICENT BOYCOTT of Mrs. Kendal, Mr. Kendal's LORD KENGUSSIE, and Mr. Hare's BARON CROODLE are still remembered. Mr. Stephenson's *Impulse* (*La Maison du Mari*), though finely acted, was not wholly sympathetic. *The Iron Master* (*Le Maitre de Forges*), by Mr. Pinero, was also but moderately sympathetic, but was excellently played and was a complete success. Mrs. Kendal as the heroine CLAIRE DE BEAUPRÉ, Mr. Kendal as PHILIPPE DERBLAY, Mr. Henley as the DUC DE BLIGNY, Mr. George Alexander as the MARQUIS DE BEAUPRÉ, Mr. Herbert Waring as the BARON DE PRÉFONT, and Miss Linda Dietz as the BARONNE DE PRÉFONT made up a superb cast. Mr. Hare then appeared as TOUCHSTONE in *As You Like It* to the ORLANDO of Mr. Kendal, the ROSALIND of Mrs. Kendal, Mr. Vezin's JAQUES, Mr. Waring's OLIVER, and Mr. Brandon Thomas's first LORD. *Mayfair*, an adaptation of *Maison Neuve*, was too Parisian in tone to suit English tastes. Mr. Pinero's *Hobby Horse*, introduced on the 25th October, 1886, depicted with moderate success some wild theories of philanthropy, and provided Mr. Hare with a part as MR. SPENCER JERMYN, a benign sportsman, which gave a pretaste of what he was to show in *A Pair of Spectacles*. Mrs. Kendal was a matron greatly daring in her charitable experiments, Mrs. Tree was a designing minx not wholly unlike Thackeray's Becky Sharp, Mr. Herbert Waring was a model clergyman, and Miss Webster an *ingénue*. Capital pictures of broken-down jockeys were presented by Mr. Mackintosh and Mr. Hendrie. The management ended on the 21st July, 1888. Successive pieces had established the reputation of Mr. and Mrs. Kendal, which, however, had never been in doubt since their splendid performances years previously at the old Prince of Wales's in *Peril* and *Diplomacy*. It needed an American tour to reveal the extent and quality of Mr. Kendal's gifts and endowments, which, however, had been—to those who took an enlightened interest in the stage— no more dubious than those of his brilliant wife. As a hero of romantic comedy Mr. Kendal has no superior. Though suspended at this time, the connection of Mr. and Mrs. Kendal with the St. James's was not ended, and on the 22nd September, 1898, while still in the flush of their American triumph, they reappeared in *The Elder Miss Blossom* of Messrs. Hendrie and Metcalfe Wood, and once more took London by storm. Before that time was reached many plays of importance had been seen.

The Dean's Daughter of Messrs. Grundy and Phillips had a strong but repellent story, and was well interpreted by Miss Olga Nethersole and a cast comprising Mr. Rutland Barrington, as a sensual and cynical clergyman, Miss Caroline Hill, Miss Adrienne Dairolles, Mr. Allan Aynesworth, Mr. Beauchamp, Mr. Waller, and Mr. Dodsworth. *Brantlingham Hall*, a serious drama by Mr. Gilbert, showed Miss Julia Neilson as a devoted and self-abnegating heroine, Mr. Nutcombe Gould in one of his admirable pictures of noblemen, Mr. Waller as a vindictive lover, Miss Rose Norreys, Mr.

THE STAGE IN THE YEAR 1900: A SOUVENIR.

Norman Forbes and Mr. Barrington. *Esther Sandraz*, a painful but dramatic adaptation by Mr. Grundy, first seen at the Prince of Wales's on the 11th June, 1889, and finely supported by Arthur Dacre and Amy Roselle, whose sad fate was not then to be anticipated, exhibited an excellent piece of acting by Mr. Fred Terry, and included among its supporters Messrs. Kemble and Brookfield and Miss Rose Leclercq. The part of the heroine was taken at the St. James's by Mrs Langtry, who, besides playing it, also appeared as ROSALIND in a revival of *As You Like It*. In this Mr. Arthur Bourchier was JAQUES, Mr. Lawrence Cautley ORLANDO, Mr. Charles Sugden TOUCHSTONE, Miss Beatrice Lamb PHEBE, and Miss Marion Lea AUDREY. Mr. Carton's amiable and graceful *Sunlight and Shadow*—most pleasingly rendered by Miss Marion Terry, Miss Maude Millett, Mr. Nutcombe Gould, Mr. Yorke Stephens, Mr. Alexander and Mr. Ben Webster—was transferred to the St. James's from the Avenue.

The Idler of Mr. Haddon Chambers, a melodramatic but stimulating play from America, produced on the 26th February, 1891, marks an epoch in the fortunes of the house. Mr.

Alexander for the first time played a leading and very difficult part in the theatre subsequently associated with his name, Miss Marion Terry gave a superbly womanly rendering of the heroine, Lady Monckton, Miss Gertrude Kingston and Miss Millett made strides upward in their profession, Mr. Waring and Mr. Nutcombe Gould enhanced their reputations, and Mr. John Mason, an American, made a prosperous *début*. In spite of a fine performance by what had now become a famous company, *Lord Anerley*, by Messrs. Hamilton and Quinton, proved too melodramatic. *Lady Windermere's Fan*, by Oscar Wilde, was the first in date of many strikingly clever and cynical pieces given by the same author. Miss Marion Terry played in it brilliantly a new type of a *femme déclassée*, and Mr. Alexander perhaps for the first time showed the sort of benignant, humorous and tender tolerance of which he is master. Miss Lily Hanbury as a wife believing herself wronged, Miss Fanny Coleman, Miss Laura Graves, Mr. Gould, Mr. Vane Tempest and Mr. Ben Webster made up an attractive cast. Mr. W. L. Courtney's poetical and tragic *Kit Marlowe* revealed Mr. Alexander as the poet-hero. *Liberty Hall*, another

THE STAGE IN THE YEAR 1900: A SOUVENIR.

delightful Dickensian play of Mr. Carton, enchanted London. Mr. Righton's old bookseller was a most lovable creature; Mr. Alexander played once more the most benevolent and benign of heroes; Mr. Webster, Mr. Gould, Mr. Vincent, Miss Maude Millett, Miss Marion Terry, Miss Coleman and Miss Ailsa Craig preserved the tender atmosphere of the old Holborn bookshop.

Mr. Alexander had assigned to his pieces such careful *mise en scène* and so admirable interpretations that his theatre was now counted as one of the foremost in existence. House and management—and, let us say, public—were ready. All that was wanting was a great play. This, too, came exactly from the source from which it might have been expected, establishing permanently and beyond the possibility of a doubt many things, among them that we had obtained at last a drama worthy of our newly developed and enlightened stage management, and last, and perhaps most important of all, an art-loving public. How far the Scandinavian stage had influenced the dramatic development we are beginning to contemplate has been much debated, without the last word having been said. That last word will not be spoken here. At any rate, *The*

Second Mrs. Tanqueray took at once its place as the greatest production of any of the St. James's managements and as one of the masterpieces of the closing years of the nineteenth century. No profit attends further analysis or criticism of a work that, after provoking wild outcry, has soared triumphant over all opposition. The problem it proposes can never lose its interest. Its treatment by the dramatist is masterly in breadth and in contrast; and every scene in it, from its delightfully peaceful and human beginning, admirably calculated to pique curiosity to its fateful close, delighted, impassioned, and harrowed the public. Mrs. Patrick Campbell as the heroine rose at once to fame, Mr. Alexander placed the seal on his high reputation, and Misses Millett, Roselle and Edith Chester, Mr. Vane Tempest, Mr. Maude, Mr. Webster and Mr. Nutcombe Gould gave the whole a representation that dwells to this day in public memory.

Speculation was rife as to the class of piece with which Mr. Alexander would follow up this startling production. Its successor proved to be *The Masqueraders* of Mr. Henry Arthur Jones, a daring, original and dramatic work, strikingly blending fantasy of conception with realism of execution. It led in the penultimate act to one of the most thrilling situations to be recalled. Unfortunately, it must be held, when Mr. Jones had depicted one of the most signal and dearly-won triumphs of love— a thing memorable in Cupid's calendar, full as this is of such—he abandoned his ground, allowed ethical considerations to triumph over the impetuosity of passion, consequently mocking the sympathies of his audience, and sent his heroine home in solitude to mourn her past follies and to sin no more. The work was an emphatic success. Mrs. Campbell first, and subsequently Miss Evelyn Millard, displayed great fascination as the barmaid-heroine; Mr. Alexander's star-gazing hero had a quiet, resolute tenderness that was worthy of the actor's best traditions; and Mr. Herbert Waring played carefully and satisfactorily a difficult part. The perfect rendering we had learnt to expect was supplied by Messrs. Elliott, Esmond, Ian Robertson, Vane Tempest and Miss Granville, while Miss Irene Vanbrugh made a stride towards the position she has since occupied. Many of the same actors, together with Miss Marion Terry, took part in the *Guy Domville* of Mr. Henry James, a piece too delicate and fragrant for our roughly-trained pit and gallery, and one which in spite of its merits and those of an admirable rendering, obtained a churlish and an inhospitable reception.

Treading closely on the heels of *Guy Domville* came Oscar Wilde's amusing trifle *The Importance of Being Earnest*, a piece at once provoking, exhilarating and frivolous. In this Mr. Allan Aynesworth showed unmistakable power in light comedy, Mr. Alexander acted with customary brightness and earnestness, Miss Evelyn Millard maintained her reputation, and Miss Irene Vanbrugh enhanced her rapidly growing fame. This work, so far as the public was concerned, was prematurely withdrawn, making way for Mr. Henry Arthur Jones's *Triumph of the Philistines*. In one sense this play might be accepted as a species of counterpart to its predecessor, since it illustrated the importance, or at least the advantage, of *not* being too earnest. Mr. Jones's satire of the Puritan dignitaries of Market Pewbury was too relentless, and in his desire to paint Philistine narrowness he let the sympathies of the public "go by the board." Poor Miss Juliette Nesville, whose premature death followed shortly afterwards, gave a striking picture of a model who is also a *cocotte*; Lady Monckton and Miss Elliott Page joined the company, and Messrs. Alexander, Waring,

THE STAGE IN THE YEAR 1900: A SOUVENIR.

Robson, Hendrie, Royston, Welch and Vincent presented a gallery of powerfully drawn eccentrics. Two plays by Mr. H. V. Esmond, conscientiously produced, revealed the possession of remarkable gifts by the young actor-dramatist. *Bogey*, the principal parts in which were played by the author and Miss Eva Moore, was too fantastic for public tastes; while *The Divided Way*, like much work by our younger dramatists, was too gloomy. In the latter piece, however, there was strong dramatic grip, and fine parts were provided for Mr. Alexander and Miss Millard, Mr. Vernon and Mr. Allan Aynesworth.

An altogether new line was opened out in *The Prisoner of Zenda*, a rendering by Mr. Edward Rose of Anthony Hope's brilliant and romantic novel. The play exactly hit the public taste, at that time running strangely in favour of romanticism. Mr. Rose's prologue, showing the origin of the resemblance between the King of Ruritania and the English house of Rassendyll, was a delightful bit of comedy of *cape et épée*, and the performances of the hero and heroine by Mr. Alexander and Miss Millard were tender and sympathetic. Mr. Vernon gave a remarkable picture of COLONEL SAPT, Mr. Herbert Waring was MICHAEL, and Misses Lily

Hanbury and Olga Brandon, Messrs. Royston, Cautley, Aynesworth, Day, Loraine, G. P. Hawtrey and George Bancroft gave all possible vivacity to what, without being a good play, was a highly agreeable entertainment. The piece was first seen 7th January, 1896; *Rupert of Hentzau*, a continuation by Anthony Hope, presented 1st Febuary, 1900, may conveniently be associated with it. In this Mr. Alexander and Mr. Vernon resumed their old parts. Miss Fay Davis succeeded Miss Millard as PRINCESS, now QUEEN, FLAVIA, and Miss Julie Opp, Miss Esmé Beringer, Mr. H. B. Irving, Mr. Esmond, Mr. Sydney Brough, and Mr. Basset Roe, replaced previous interpreters. Like most sequences it was less popular than the preceding work. *Mary Pennington, Spinster*, a comedy with much promise of Mr. W. R. Walkes, served for the introduction on the stage of Miss Mary Jerrold, a pleasing young actress, and was given for a solitary occasion by Miss Olga Brandon, Miss Kate Rorke, Mr. Cyril Maude, and Mr. Sydney Brough.

After a poetical and effective performance of *As You Like It*—with Mr. Alexander as ORLANDO, Mr. Vernon as JAQUES, Mr. Fernandez as the DUKE, Mr. Aubrey Smith as FREDERICK, Mr. H. B. Irving as

THE STAGE IN THE YEAR 1900: A SOUVENIR.

OLIVER, Mr. Esmond as TOUCHSTONE, Miss Julia Neilson as ROSALIND, Miss Fay Davis as CELIA, Miss Dorothea Baird as PHEBE, Miss Julie Opp as HYMEN, and Miss Kate Phillips as AUDREY—the management produced Mr. Pinero's sparkling comedy *The Princess and the Butterfly*. This is the best of many plays vindicating the right of the man of middle age to indulge in the luxury of seeking to be loved for his own sake. The thesis is maintained with all Mr. Pinero's brilliancy. SIR GEORGE LENORMANT is one of Mr. Alexander's best parts, and the FAY ZULIANI of Miss Fay Davis is, with the exception of MRS. FLOYD in *A Debt of Honour*, that winsome actress's best character. The love scenes between the two were full of fragrance. Not less effective were those between Miss Julia Neilson and Mr. H. B. Irving. Mrs. Cecil Raleigh, forsaking melodrama for comedy, Miss Rose Leclercq, Miss Julie Opp, Miss Mabel Hackney, Messrs. Aubrey Smith, Esmond, Vincent, George Bancroft, Vane Tempest and Royston kept up worthily the tradition of the house and supplied a finished representation of a piece which, though "caviare to the general," was the delight of the gourmet. *The Tree of Knowledge* of Mr. Carton has a profoundly interesting story and is written with literary finish, but is more conventional and less idyllic in treatment than its author's ordinary work. It found Miss Julia Neilson an original part as a thoroughly bad woman, which she played in capital style. Mr. Alexander was also well suited. The cast supplied included Miss Carlotta Addison, Miss Winifred Dolan, and Messrs. Vernon, Fred Terry, H. B. Irving, Esmond, and Shelton. *The Conquerors* of Mr. Paul M. Potter, founded upon the *Mademoiselle Fifi* of Guy de Maupassant, and, it is said, on other tales of the same author, gave the theatre an unfamiliar air of melodrama. The company, headed by Mr. Alexander and Miss Fay Davis, Miss Julia Neilson and Messrs. F. Terry, Vernon, H. B. Irving, and Esmond, played the piece for all and more than all it was worth.

The Ambassador of John Oliver Hobbes, 2nd June, 1898, introduced to the St. James's a new and charming comedy, and practically to the stage a dramatist of distinguished abilities. Mrs. Craigie's comedy is delightful alike in dialogue and characterisation; and the love scenes between LORD ST. ORBYN, beautifully played by Mr. Alexander, and JULIET GAINSBOROUGH, no less refreshingly played

THE STAGE IN THE YEAR 1900: A SOUVENIR.

by Miss Fay Davis, were in themselves enough to secure the success of the entertainment. Mr. H. B. Irving as SIR WILLIAM BEAUVEDERE, a grave, solemn and fatuous diplomat, Miss Violet Vanbrugh, and Miss Granville, gave fine pieces of comedy acting; Mr. F. Terry was excellent as a bluff major and man of the world, and Mr. Esmond was an incautious youth. Superbly mounted and no less superbly played the piece won a triumph. It was succeeded the following year by *In Days of Old*, a romantic, quasi-historical drama by Mr. Edward Rose, dealing with a supposed episode of the Wars of the Roses and introducing King Henry VI and Queen Margaret. This constituted a brilliant spectacle, was acted to perfection, and supplied Mr. Alexander with a part more heroic and soldierly than he often essays. After *Rupert of Hentzau* came *The Man of Forty*, by Mr. Walter Frith, a piece which, after being given in the country, underwent a process of transformation which emphatically deprived of vraisemblance a portion of the action. Mr. H. B. Irving had a double *rôle*, a sort of faint reflection of Dubosc and Lesurques, in which he scored. Mr. Alexander, Mr. Aubrey Smith, Miss Fay Davis, Miss Carlotta Addison, Miss Esmé Beringer, Miss

Granville, and Mrs. Maesmore Morris were well fitted, and the whole was sympathetic and interesting. With the summer season of 1900 came Mr. Grundy's *Debt of Honour*, an alteration or enlargement of a piece of the same author previously seen. This found employment for Mr. Alexander and the whole of his distinguished company, and exhibited some earnest and pathetic acting by Miss Fay Davis, together with a pretty picture of worthy and beautiful womanhood by Miss Julie Opp. To it was afterwards joined as an epilogue, *In Honour Bound*, a one-act piece of Mr. Grundy, which also had been seen before. The latest production at the St. James's has consisted of Mrs. Craigie's *The Wisdom of the Wise*, a pretty and delicate piece, rather too thin for modern requirements.

CHAPTER X.

OPENED in 1882, it has been alleged, rather as a mercantile than as a histrionic speculation, in the expectation that the site would soon be indispensable to the Charing Cross railway station, the Avenue had a diversified and, at the outset, unsatisfactory experience. Its earliest ventures were in comic opera and vaudeville, and its chief attractions consisted in the performances of Miss Florence St. John —who with a happier training might have been an English Judic—and M. Marius. An attempt at serious drama was made in *The Struggle for Life*, adapted from M. Daudet's *La Lutte pour la Vie* by Messrs. Robert Buchanan and Fred Horner. This rather gloomy piece, first seen in 1890, was well played by Mr. Alexander, Mr. Fred Kerr, Miss Alma Stanley, Miss Kate Phillips, Miss Louisa Graves, and Miss Geneviève Ward. *Sunlight and Shadow*, by Mr. R. C. Carton, a touching and effective play, supplied Mr. George Alexander with a part of sublime self-sacrifice, and gave opportunities to Messrs. Nutcombe Gould, Yorke Stephens, Miss Marion Terry, and Miss Maude Millett. *The Henrietta* of Mr. Bronson Howard, a powerful play and a brilliant satire, had ill-luck, and in spite of a capable interpretation by Messrs. Yorke Stephens, Vernon, Waller, Shine, Miss Fanny Brough and Miss Florence West, had no very long life. Mr. Henry Arthur Jones produced under his own direction his comedy *The Crusaders*. The spell of the house was upon the work, and though admirable alike in dialogue and characterisation, as satire and as play, and acted with an *ensemble* then rarely surpassed, it obtained no more than a *succès d'estime*. Lady Monckton, Miss Emery, Miss Olga Brandon, Miss Lillie Belmore, Messrs. Arthur Cecil, Yorke Stephens, Lewis Waller, Kemble, Sant Matthews and Allan Aynesworth took part in an ideal interpretation. After the production of Mr. A. C. Calmour's *Bread Winner* and revivals of *Judah, A Doll's House, Forget-me-Not, A White Lie* and *The Iron Master*, came some very interesting but not too successful experiments—Dr. Todhunter's *Comedy of Sighs*, Mr. Yeates's *Land of Heart's Desire*, and Mr. Bernard

Shaw's *Arms and the Man*. The work last named, a piece of finished satire, constituted an admirably humorous entertainment. It was well played by Mr. Yorke Stephens, Mr. Bernard Gould, Mr. Welch, and Miss Alma Murray. On the 2nd November, 1895 Mr. Charles Hawtrey appeared at the theatre, the fortune of which he has made, playing in Mr. Burnand's *Mrs. Ponderbury's Past*.

Nelson's Enchantress, by Risden Home, introduced for the first time, on the 11th February, 1897, Mr. Forbes-Robertson to the Avenue. Mr. Robertson's make-up as the hero of Trafalgar was a triumph as remarkable as was the NAPOLEON of Sir Henry Irving at the Lyceum a month or two later. Mrs. Patrick Campbell realised many attractive aspects of LADY HAMILTON, but the other parts need not be enumerated. Mr. Frederick Horner's *On Leave* and Mr. Lumley's *Belle Bellair*, with shorter pieces by Sir Charles Young, Mrs. Oscar Beringer and others, together with a performance by the New Century theatre of *Admiral Guinea*, by Messrs. Henley and Stevenson, belong to the same year. In *Belle Bellair*, Mrs. John Wood, Miss Irene Vanbrugh, Mr. Weedon Grossmith and Mr. Martin Harvey took part. *Admiral Guinea* was powerfully rendered by Mr. Mollison, Mr. Sydney Valentine, Mr. R. Loraine, Miss Cissie Loftus and Miss Dolores Drummond. *Sweet Nancy* by Mr. Buchanan, and *A Bit of Old Chelsea* by Mrs. Oscar Beringer, were revived, *Lord and Lady Algy* was transferred from the Comedy, and *The Cuckoo*, a clever adaptation by Mr. Brookfield of *Décoré*, was given before the greatest triumph the house has known was obtained with Mr. Ganthony's *Message from Mars*. This fantasy, in which Mr. Hawtrey is unsurpassable, is still running, and bids fair to eclipse in popularity any piece of recent days.

On the 18th January, 1884, Mr. Edgar Bruce opened the Prince's theatre, which soon afterwards, not without some possibilities of confusing future historians of the stage, was renamed the "Prince of Wales's." Performances began with a revival of Mr. Gilbert's *Palace of Truth* and Mr. Grundy's *In Honour Bound*. *Breaking a Butterfly*, an alteration by Messrs. Jones and Herman of *A Doll's House*, came before the Ibsen cult was established. Though well supported by Mr. Tree as the Rev. Robert Spalding, Misses Tilbury and Lucy Buckstone, and other well-known actors and actresses,

The Private Secretary, adapted from the *Bibliothekar* of Herr Von Moser by Mr. C. H. Hawtrey, was almost if not quite a failure. None, at least, foresaw the brilliant success it was subsequently to attain at the Globe. In Mr. Comyns Carr's workmanlike version of Hugh Conway's *Called Back*, Mr. Tree made one of his first great effects on the stage. His PAOLO MACARI was a weird and powerful piece of acting, and Miss Lingard as PAULINE, Mr. Kyrle Bellew as GILBERT VAUGHAN, Mr. G. W. Anson, and other actors, won recognition.

Mr. Coghlan's rendering of *La Princesse Georges* showed the adapter as the PRINCE, Mrs. Langtry as SÉVÉRINE, Mr. Somerset as the COMTE DE TERREMONDE, Mrs. Billington, and Miss Rosina Filippi, and was not a success. Mr. Norman Forbes appeared in Wills's rendering of *Gringoire*. In *Enemies*—a translation of *La Grande Marnière*—Mr. Coghlan, the adapter, was RICHARD DARVEL, and Mrs. Langtry MARGARET GLENN, Mr. Kemble, Mr. Fernandez and Mr. Pateman being in the cast. Mr. Boucicault, supported by Miss Myra Holme, Mr. Graham, Mr. J. G. Taylor and Mr. Billington, appeared in his sporting drama *The Jilt*. First produced at an afternoon presentation on the 23rd February, 1888, Mr. Seebohm's adaptation of Mrs. Burnett's *Little Lord Fauntleroy* enchanted the public, and has since been often seen. A delightful interpretation by Miss Annie Hughes as Cedric Errol, Mr. Somerset as the Earl, Miss Mary Rorke as " Dearest," and Mr. Arthur Williams as Mr. Hobbs, commended it warmly and deservedly to the public.

Pélléas and Mélisande, produced 21st June, 1898, introduced to this house Mr. Forbes-Robertson, Mr. Martin Harvey, and Mrs. Patrick Campbell. This masterpiece of the mystical drama was fairly rendered; Mrs. Campbell giving a poetical and plaintive rendering of the heroine, Mr. Robertson as Golaud being inspired by the very spirit of romance, and Mr. Martin Harvey realising picturesquely the helplessness of Mélisande's boy lover. Scarcely less mystic than this piece was *The Moonlight Blossom*, a Japanese romance by Mr. Chester Bailey Fernald. In this Mrs. Patrick Campbell played with much subtlety the heroine, and Mr. Forbes-Robertson allowed himself to be seen in a part wholly unworthy of his eminent gifts. Revenge for this was taken by Mr. Robertson in *The Sacrament of Judas*, adapted by Mr. Louis N. Parker from

THE STAGE IN THE YEAR 1900: A SOUVENIR.

M. Tiercelin. His performance of JACQUES BERNEZ —the renegade priest, over whom vows and former associations exercise so potent an influence and whose self-sacrifice is so sublime—was a magnificent piece of interpretation. Mrs. Patrick Campbell was JEFFIK GUILLON, the heroine. *The Canary*, by George Flemming, in which Mrs. Campbell appeared without the assistance of Mr. Robertson, was a brilliantly humorous and attractive play, which a clever piece of acting by Mrs. Campbell raised to the height of popularity. Mr. Garden, Mr. Du Maurier, Mr. Yorke Stephens and Mr. Bromley Davenport took part in an excellent performance, and the play was removed to the Royalty to finish its run, making room for *The Only Way* of Mr. Freeman Wills, transferred from the Lyceum. In this piece Mr. Martin Harvey—already known for his romantic assumptions, showed his command of pathos, presenting a most touching picture of SYDNEY CARTON. Miss Grace Warner was the original exponent of LUCY MANETTE, and Miss De Silva, Miss Marriott, Miss Lizzie Webster, Mr. Holbrook Blinn, Mr. J. G. Taylor, Mr. B. Webster and Mr. Everill took important parts. An adaptation of *Don Juan de Maraña*, in which Mr. Harvey was subsequently seen, though interesting to students, failed quite to hit the public taste, the rendering being inexpert and the character of the hero unduly idealised. It was succeeded by a triple bill, the most attractive item in which, *Ib and Little Chrictina*, was musical rather than dramatic.

On the 21st August, 1900, Miss Marie Tempest made her *début* in comedy as NELL GYWN in the *English Nell* of Anthony Hope and Mr. Edward Rose. Her performance of the orange girl promoted to be the mistress of a king was admirable in vivacity and piquancy, and proved the actress to be a genuine comedian. Mr. F. Cooper gave a good presentation of CHARLES II, and Miss Lily Hanbury, Mrs. Sam Sothern, Mr. Ben Webster and Mr. Fuller Mellish aided in securing a triumph for a piece that was pleasant enough but scarcely strong. Comparisons between this piece and *Sweet Nell of Old Drury*, at the Haymarket, were necessarily numerous.

On the 17th October, 1887, with *The Churchwarden*, a farce from the German which had already had a run at the Olympic, Mr. Terry opened the theatre in the Strand which bears his name and has been intimately associated with his fortunes. The success of the piece was renewed and the house witnessed many subsequent comedies and farces, as a rule of the lightest though sometimes of the most exhilarating description; one or two pieces by Mr. Pinero in his happiest vein to which Mr. Terry—an eccentric comedian if ever there was one entitled to be so called—did full justice, elevating the house in public estimation. The first great triumph was obtained with Mr. Pinero's *Sweet Lavender*, a comedy telling a singularly touching tale, and exhibiting Mr. Terry in the part of a dissipated and bibulous barrister, a character in which he has since often been seen, and always to the highest advantage. The comedy was not only the best Mr. Terry has produced during his tenancy of the house, it was also the best acted. Misses Norreys, Maude Millett, M. A. Victor and Carlotta Addison, and Messrs. Brandon Thomas, Bernard Gould, Alfred Bishop, Terry, F. Kerr, Sant Matthews and Valentine constituted an absolutely exemplary cast.

The Real Little Lord Fauntleroy, by Mrs. Hodgson Burnett, introduced the two Miss Beringers, Miss Winifred Emery, Miss Fanny Brough, and Messrs. Bishop, Brandon Thomas, Albert Chevalier, and Hendrie. Its success was overshadowed by that of the previous and, as was stated, unauthorised version.

Mr. Pigott's *Bookmaker* provided Mr. Terry with a comic part as a bookmaker who unexpectedly becomes a baronet. The play enjoyed a good deal of popularity, and would have enjoyed more had the female characters been more strongly cast. *New Lamps for Old*, by Mr. Jerome, showed Mr. Penley at Terry's theatre as an ill-used solicitor, and had parts for Miss Gertrude Kingston, Miss Cissie Grahame, Mr. Bernard Gould and Mr. F. Kerr. *In Chancery*, by Mr. Pinero, transferred from the Gaiety and the Olympic, had an aftermath of success. Mr. Penley was also seen in Mr. Arthur Law's farce *The Judge*. A triple bill, the first of a kind that soon sprang into popularity, consisted of *The Lancashire Sailor*, a tender piece by Mr. Brandon Thomas, *A Commission*, a comic sketch by Mr. Weedon Grossmith, in which that whimsical comedian was seen to great advantage, and *A Pantomime Rehearsal*, by Mr. Cecil Clay, which enjoyed immense popularity at different houses and with varying casts. These pieces were soon transferred to the Shaftesbury, making room for Mr. Pinero's comedy *The Times*. Though rather more serious than previous works from the same source, and showing Mr. Terry in a part sentimental rather than comic, *The Times*, played by Miss Fanny Brough, Miss Annie Hill, Messrs. Lovell, Elliott, Esmond and F. Thorne, enjoyed much popularity. It counts among the few conspicuous successes of the theatre. *Gudgeons*, by Messrs. Louis N. Parker and Thornton Clark, introduced two clever satirical characters to which justice was done by Mr. Waring and Miss Janette Steer. *The New Boy*, of Mr. Arthur Law, showed Mr. Weedon Grossmith in a very comic part of a man of ripe years compelled to pass as a schoolboy. *The Blue Boar*, by Messrs. Louis N. Parker and Thornton Clark, also presented Mr. Terry in a rôle suited to his idiosyncrasy. *The Passport* of Messrs. Yardley and B. C. Stephenson, produced at Terry's and then transferred to the Trafalgar, was a delightful piece of fooling. *Jedbury, Junior*, a curiously nondescript piece by Mrs. Madeleine Lucette Ryley, was admirably played by Miss Maude Millett and Miss Eva Moore, Mr. F. Kerr, Mr. Beauchamp, Mr. Playfair, and Mr. Gilbert Farquhar. *Love in Idleness*, a slight but pretty

comedy by Mr. Louis N. Parker and Mr. Edward
J. Goodman, exhibited Mr. Terry as a man who
exchanges habits of indolent *laissez faire* for others
of undue activity. Miss Bella Pateman reappeared
in this, as did also Miss Beatrice Ferrar. Mr.
Gilbert Farquhar scored as a member of Parliament
and Mr. de Lange as a peppery Frenchman.

Plays subsequently seen included *The White
Knight* by Mr. Stuart Ogilvie, *The Broad Road* by
Captain Robert Marshall, *The Brixton Burglary* by
Mr. F. W. Sydney, *What will the World Say?* by Mr.
G. P. Bancroft, *The Weather Hen* by Messrs. Berte
Thomas and Granville Barker, *The Lady of Ostend*
by Mr. F. C. Burnand, *Captain Birchell's Luck* by
Mr. Louis N. Parker, and *The Heather Field*, a play
of serious interest by Mr. Edward Martyn, given as
an experiment of the Irish Literary Society.

The Shaftesbury opened with *As You Like It* on
the 20th October, 1888, under the management of
Mr. John Lancaster. Accustomed to cater for a
Manchester public Mr. Lancaster was at first not too
successful in London. Miss Wallis (Mrs. Lancaster)
played agreeably as ROSALIND, Mr. Forbes-Robertson
was ORLANDO, Mr. William Farren ADAM, Mr.
Mackintosh TOUCHSTONE, and Mr. Arthur Stirling

JAQUES. *Calumny*, from the Spanish of *Don José Echegaray*, by Mr. Malcolm Watson, came the following year.

Mr. Henry Arthur Jones's play, *The Middleman*, brought with it into the house an overpowering burst of sunshine. One of the best of Mr. Jones's serious works, it was acted splendidly by Mr. Willard as the enthusiastic potter, whom a sense of injustice and wrong converts into an avenging angel. Mr. Mackintosh, Mr. Esmond, Miss Annie Hughes, Miss Maude Millett, and Miss Eva Moore, shared in a triumph in its line the most conspicuous the theatre has known. After playing in Mr. Law's *Dick Venables*, Mr. Willard scored yet another success in Mr. Jones's *Judah* given on 21st May, 1890. Mr. Willard's WELSH PRIEST is perhaps the best part in which he has been seen. The general cast was once more excellent, and the VASHTI of Miss Olga Brandon, the LADY EVE of Miss Bessie Hatton, Miss Gertrude Warden's MISS JOPP, Mr. Sant Matthews's PROFESSOR JOPP, Mr. C. Fulton's EARL OF ASGARBY, Mr. Royce Carleton's MR. DETHIC, and Mr. F. Kerr's JUXON PRALL, contributed to make the piece one of the most popular of the day. Mr. Lewis Waller, Miss Norreys, Miss Annie Hill, and Miss Fanny Coleman, appeared in a pretty one-act piece of Mr. Jones's, *Sweet Will*, and Mr. Willard in *The Deacon*, a two-act piece of the same author. Musical comedy or comic opera became then the chief support of the house which returned to drama, however, with *The Manxman*, adapted by Mr. Hall Caine from his own novel. In this version the interest, to the great detriment of the play, was transferred from PETE to PHILIP CHRISTIAN. Mr. Lewis Waller was the new hero, and Miss Florence West the heroine, the cast comprising Mr. Fernandez, Mr. Brookfield, Mr. Kemble, Mr. Hamilton Knight, and Miss Kate Phillips. *The Sin of St. Hulda*, a romantic, religious, and to some extent historical play, by Mr. Stuart Ogilvie, was capitally rendered by Miss Kate Rorke and Mr. Charles Cartwright. In a not very brilliant adaptation of *The Sorrows of Satan*, Mr. Lewis Waller made a resplendent fiend. *Sporting Life*, a vivacious drama by Messrs. Cecil Raleigh and Seymour Hicks, closes the dramatic record of a house that has risen to fortune on the strength of musical productions.

On the 17th December of the same year the Lyric opened, under the management of Mr. H. J.

THE STAGE IN THE YEAR 1900: A SOUVENIR.

Leslie, with the opera of *Dorothy*, transferred from the Prince of Wales's. As was to be expected from its name, the house has, in the main, confined itself to music. Its first dramatic venture was *Sweet Nancy*, an adaptation from Miss Rhoda Broughton, given on the 12th July, which was one of the daintiest pieces of the day. Mr. Henry Neville was the original SIR ROGER TEMPEST, Miss Harriet Jay BARBARA GREY, and Mr. Esmond ALGERNON. As the youngsters, Miss Annie Hughes, Miss Beatrice Ferrar, Mr. Hallard, and others, were irresistible. On the 4th January, 1896, the house reached the height of its success with *The Sign of the Cross* of Mr. Wilson Barrett. It is useless to revive the contest concerning this piece, which, while it obtained the enthusiastic applause of ecclesiastics from the episcopate downwards, had to face the strongest arraignment of criticism upon the very points on which the Church should be able to speak with most authority. The contrast between Pagan and Christian civilisation has much that is striking, picturesque and suggestive, as is known to scholars and seen in the novel of *Quo Vadis*, and the adaptation of it that has been put on the stage. Mr. Barrett as MARCUS SUPERBUS, Mr. Franklin McLeay as NERO, Miss Grace Warner as POPPÆA, Miss Maud Jeffries as MERCIA, the Christian maiden, and Miss Haidée Wright as a juvenile martyr, were very popular, and the piece, which had effective situations, was the most discussed that the present generation has known. As to the fidelity of the pictures of Christian life under the Roman Emperors, if the Church is satisfied what more need be said? As a contribution to literature the play was not noteworthy, and there were points in the *mise en scène* that justified objection. A version of *The Manxman*, preferable to that at the Shaftesbury, was played without interrupting the run of *The Sign of the Cross*. In this Mr. Barrett gave a touching picture of the honest-hearted and devoted PETE, and Miss Jeffries was acceptable as KATE CREEGAN. *The Waters of Babylon* constituted a lovely spectacle, and was well acted by Mr. Barrett, Mr. Franklin McLeay, Miss Maud Jeffries, and Miss Lily Hanbury. It is wordy, however, and its language is unhappily distorted. It was scarcely so popular accordingly as it had been expected to be. Revivals of *Virginius* and *Othello* were given by Mr. Barrett; and Mr. Charles Bailey Fernald's *The Cat and the Cherub*, one of two versions seen in London, was produced here.

CHAPTER XI.

At a bound the Garrick sprang to the highest position in popularity and in art. Built for Mr. W. S. Gilbert, it was opened upon the 24th April, 1889, by Mr. John Hare with *The Profligate* of Mr. Pinero. A house could scarcely begin under happier auspices, and the first venture established it firmly in public regard. More serious than Mr. Pinero's previous pieces, and as inflexible in morality as the latest diatribe of the younger Dumas, *The Profligate* gave promise of, and prepared the way for, *The Second Mrs. Tanqueray*. It is true that, as a concession to English love for the "live happy ever afterwards" termination, the ending of the acting version was prosperous, while that of the printed book was fatal. Few, however, of the audience could have been in doubt as to what was Mr. Pinero's true thesis. After his old custom, Mr. Hare contented himself with the part of an elderly reprobate, and left to Mr. Forbes-Robertson the *rôle* of DUNSTAN RENSHAW, an average man of the world, who, marrying a simple, virtuous and pure-minded maiden to whom he becomes passionately attached, enforces Mr. Pinero's moral by paying with his happiness and his life for a past the iniquity of which he perceives too late. In hands better than those of this admirable actor the character could not have been, and the heroine of Miss Kate Rorke, spotless in purity, added to the attractions of the whole. Mr. Lewis Waller as HUGH MURRAY, the devoted friend of the heroine, Miss Olga Nethersole as JANET, Miss Beatrice Lamb as IRENE, and Mr. Sydney Brough as WILFRED BRUDENELL, were conspicuous features in a brilliant entertainment.

An adaptation of *La Tosca* with a memorable cast which, however, did not include Mr. Hare, followed on the 28th November, 1889. Mrs. Bernard Beere—who in Sarah Bernhardt parts has had no English rival—was the TOSCA, Mr. Lewis Waller presented powerfully CAVARADOSSI (converted from the heroine's lover into her husband), Mr. Forbes-Robertson obtained one of the most conspicuous of his triumphs as SCARPIA, and Mr. Gilbert Farquhar gave an excellent picture of aristocratic fatuousness as the MARCHESE OTTAVANTI. Other parts were supported by Miss Rose Leclercq, Miss Bessie Hatton, Messrs. Waring, S. Brough, Dodsworth, R. Cathcart, and F. H. Knight. On the 22nd February, 1890, came *A Pair of Spectacles* (an adaptation by Mr. Grundy of *Les Petits Oiseaux*), which has remained one of the most popular pieces in Mr. Hare's repertory. That actor may indeed count BENJAMIN GOLDFINCH as the most Dickens-like and cherubic part he has ever essayed. Scarcely less remarkable was the UNCLE GREGORY ("the man from Sheffield") of Mr. Groves, which is the masterpiece of that broad and unctuous actor. Miss Kate Rorke was delightful as MRS. GOLDFINCH. At the present moment this is one of the most admired of pieces, and its catchwords have become popular locutions.

Lady Bountiful, another work of Mr. Pinero, was a marvel of ingenuity, and in some scenes exhibited much pathos. It supplied Mr. Hare with a part of the HAROLD SKIMPOLE type, in which he was seen at his best. His son, Mr. Gilbert Hare, made as a baronet a first appearance in London, Mr. Forbes-Robertson was a brave and independent young hero, Mr. Groves and Miss Dolores Drummond gave good pictures of a livery stable keeper and his wife, Miss

Kate Rorke had a not too sympathetic part, and Miss Carlotta Addison, Miss Marie Linden, Miss Beatrice Ferrar, Miss Webster and Mr. Somerset were seen to some advantage. A revival of Robertson's *School* showed Mr. Gilbert Hare as KRUX, Mr. Mackintosh as the BEAU, Mr. H. B. Irving as LORD BEAUFOY, Miss Kate Rorke as BELLA, and Miss Annie Hughes as NAOMI TIGHE.

A Fool's Paradise, by Mr. Grundy, brought on Mr. Hare as a physician, Miss Olga Nethersole as a poisoner, and Misses Kate Rorke and B. Ferrar, Mr. H. B. Irving and Mr. F. Kerr in other parts.

After some experiments of no special interest *Robin Goodfellow*, a three-act play of Mr. R. C. Carton—romantic in story and sparkling with good things—was produced, Mr. Hare reappearing as VALENTINE BARBROOK, a heartless, sinister and plausible intriguer and swindler. The interest centred in two pairs of lovers, pleasantly played by Mr. Forbes-Robertson and Miss Kate Rorke, Mr. S. Brough, and Miss Rose Norreys. Miss Compton, as a woman of the world, had some cynical speeches assigned to her, and Mrs. Edmund Phelps was a venerable grandmother.

THE STAGE IN THE YEAR 1900: A SOUVENIR.

Diplomacy was then revived with a startling cast, Mr. and Mrs. Bancroft reappearing as COUNT ORLOFF and LADY HENRY FAIRFAX, Mr. Forbes-Robertson and Miss Kate Rorke obtaining an undisputed triumph as JULIAN BEAUCLERC and DORA, Mr. Hare being HENRY BEAUCLERC, Mr. Arthur Cecil BARON STEIN, Mr. Gilbert Hare ALGIE, Miss Nethersole COUNTESS ZICKA, and Lady Monckton the MARQUISE DE RIO-ZARES. At a subsequent revival in the autumn Miss Elizabeth Robins was COUNTESS ZICKA. The play had lost nothing of its grip, the new cast was equal to the old, and the revivals were received with tumultuous enthusiasm. *An Old Jew*, by Mr. Grundy, given 6th January, 1895, is a brilliant but not very accurate or judicious satire of the journalistic world. Mr. Hare gave a superb picture of a modern Hebrew Monte-Cristo, and Mr. W. L. Abingdon, Mr. Gilbert Farquhar and Mr. G. W. Anson presented very clever sketches of Bohemian eccentrics. The play, though it ran for three months, scarcely gripped the public, and made way, on the 7th April, for the *Mrs. Lessingham* of George Flemming. This first dramatic work of a clever author won favourable recognition but failed to hold its place. It was what was then known as a problem play; its heroine, admirably presented by Miss Elizabeth Robins, being contrasted with a woman of pure and noble nature, no less admirably realised by Miss Kate Rorke; Mr. Forbes-Robertson played with much firmness and power a rather thankless part of the hero; and Mr. Hare gave a fine study of character, a little out of his ordinary line, as a soldier.

Mr. Hare next produced Mr. Grundy's *Slaves of the Ring*, in which he played a crotchetty and irascible old nobleman, and was supported by Miss Kate Rorke and a company—new in part—comprising Mr. Arthur Bourchier, Mr. Brandon Thomas, Mr. G. Du Maurier, Mrs. Boucicault, Miss Kate Phillips, and Miss Eleanor Calhoun. It made way on the 13th May, 1895, for *The Notorious Mrs. Ebbsmith* of Mr. Pinero, one of the greatest, albeit the most fiercely contested, plays of its epoch, and the greatest triumph of Mr. Hare's management. Worshipped by the upholders of the new school, it was the culminating product of its class, and by its very popularity prepared the way for that reaction towards the romantic drama which was a curious and passing phase of the closing years of the century. As a type of the woman in revolt against restrictions, social and theological, Mrs. Patrick Campbell rose to the height of her reputation, Mr. Forbes-Robertson assigned all possible depth and subtlety to LUCAS CLEEVE, and Mr. Hare outdid himself as the DUKE OF ST. OLPHERTS. Miss Ellis Jeffreys, Miss Calhoun, Mr. Ian Robertson and Mr. Aubrey Smith were included in an exemplary cast. Epoch-marking in almost every sense the play was, though it is characteristic of the conservatism and timidity of English character that the epoch seems past. Of problem plays this was the greatest and practically the last.

Mr. Jerome's *Rise of Dick Halward* brought back Mr. Willard, who acted the hero, and was supported by Miss Marion Terry, Miss Annie Hughes, Mr. Barnes, and Mr. Esmond. In *Alabama*, an importation from America, Mr. Willard and Miss Marion Terry had previously been seen with Miss Keith Wakeman, Miss Agnes Miller, and Mr. Fernandez. In *The Rogue's Comedy* of Mr. Jones, a brilliant satire of social institutions, played on the 21st April, 1896, Mr. Willard strengthened his reputation, exhibiting an impostor whose career of successful dishonesty is checked by his son, the one being in the world for whose affection he pines. A powerful and pathetic idea was excellently wrought by both dramatist and actor. Mr. Lovell as the son, and Miss Olliffe as the accomplice and wife of the swindler, contributed to the success.

The next tenants of the Garrick were Mr. and Mrs. Kendal, who, on the 10th June, transferred thither from the country *The Greatest of These*, a piece the serious, dignified elevation and pathos of which enable it to dispute with *Sowing the Wind* the position of Mr. Grundy's masterpiece. Mrs. Kendal played in masterly style as the penitent heroine, Mr. Kendal showed his power of presenting a character sterner and less sunny than he ordinarily essays, and Mr. H. Kemble was a meddlesome old clergyman. *My Friend the Prince*, by Mr. Justin Huntly McCarthy, came during a *régime* of music, and showed to advantage Miss Miriam Clements, Miss Sibyl Carlisle, and Miss Juliette Nesville, Mr. Paul Arthur, Mr. F. Kaye, Mr. Herbert Ross, and Mr. James Welch. *22a Curzon Street*, by Mr. Brandon Thomas and Mr. John Edwards, *Too Much Johnson*[*], *Sue*, taken by Mr. Pemberton from Bret Harte, in which Miss Annie Russell created a highly favourable impression, *Teresa*, by Mr. George Playdell Bancroft, transferred from the Métropole,

[*] An American adaptation of *La Plantation Thomassin* of M. Maurice Ordonneau.

THE STAGE IN THE YEAR 1900: A SOUVENIR.

Camberwell, and *Brother Officers*, by Mr. Leo Trevor, were seen in 1898, and *Change Alley*, by Messrs. Parker and Carson, and *Halves*, by Dr. A. Conan Doyle, in 1899. None of these pieces contributed greatly to the development of the drama. *A Court Scandal* was transferred from the Court, and *The Degenerates* from the Haymarket. 1900 witnessed the appearance of Mrs. Leslie Carter as ZAZA, a performance of more cleverness than charm. The latest production at this house is the pleasing *Wedding Guest* of Mr. J. M. Barrie.

To the last few years belongs the history of the Trafalgar Square, now the Duke of York's, and Daly's, theatres. The former, opened 10th September, 1892, was originally devoted to music or the lightest form of farcical comedy. As the Duke of York's it gave *Her Advocate*, by Mr. Walter Frith, a not wholly convincing play, the principal characters in which were taken by Miss Lena Ashwell, Miss Henrietta Watson, Miss Gertrude Kingston, Mr. Charles Cartwright, Mr. C. W. Somerset, Mr. Oswald Yorke, and Mr. J. H. Barnes. *The Happy Life*, a pleasing if whimsical comedy of Mr. Louis N. Parker, which began in most romantic fashion and ended less well, obtained recognition on its own merits and on a pleasing interpretation by Mr. Hermann Vezin, Mr. F. Kerr, Mr. Beauchamp, Miss Cowen, Miss Watson, and Miss Dorothea Baird. The claims of the theatre to be a first-class house for the first time fully asserted themselves with the production, on the 11th October, 1898, of Anthony Hope's charming fantasy, *The Adventures of Lady Ursula*. This delightful picture of eighteenth-century life owed much to the bewitching impersonation by Miss Evelyn Millard of LADY URSULA BARRINGTON. Her duel with SIR GEORGE SYLVESTER, well played by Mr. Herbert Waring, was a remarkable display of delicacy and finish, and her appearance generally in her boy's dress was very effective. Mr. Charles Fulton, Mr. Sam Sothern, Mr. J. C. Buckstone and Miss Agnes Miller took part in a bright performance. American pieces by an American company, headed by Mr. Nat Goodwin and Misses Maxine and Gertrude Elliott, followed. Mr. Hall Caine's powerful play, *The Christian*, furnished fine opportunities to Miss Millard, Mr. Waring, and Mr. Groves, but was not a complete success. A further triumph attended Mr. Waring and Miss Millard in Mr. Jerome's *Miss Hobbs*, in which they were supported by Mr. Allan Aynesworth, Mr.

Cosmo Stuart, Miss Agnes Miller, and Miss Susie Vaughan. Strengthened by the addition of *Madame Butterfly*, by Mr. Belasco, in which Miss Millard gave a supremely touching presentation of the Japanese heroine, this bill ran until the end of the summer season of 1900, and made way in September for *The Lackeys' Carnival* of Mr. Henry Arthur Jones, which, in spite of a few performances, did not succeed. *The Swashbuckler*, a fantasy by Mr. Louis N. Parker, now holds possession.

Daly's theatre was opened on the 27th June, 1893, by the American actor and manager whose name it bears. Short as is its career, thanks to the great ability and charm of Miss Ada Rehan and the other members of a distinguished American company which settled in our midst and took like an Embassy, the position of a portion of a foreign country established in London, it has exercised much influence, and is to be counted a valuable asset in our possessions. With a few exceptions, however, the most distinguished of which was the production of Tennyson's *Foresters*, the management confined itself at the outset to American pieces, translations principally by Daly from the German, or to revivals of Shakespeare, in which prettiness of *mise en scène* and excellence of cast had to compound, as best they might, for the most squeamish and irreverent treatment ever accorded the language of the great dramatist. In order to avoid the evils of such an example we should have been content to forego the gain that was reaped from a performance such even as that of *The Taming of the Shrew*, the beauties of which linger yet in the memory. During late years the theatre has attained unrivalled prosperity with lyrical pieces, in which the singing of Mr. Hayden Coffin, Miss Marie Tempest, Miss Lottie Venne, Miss Letty Lind, and other artists, has formed an enduring attraction. With other theatres, such as the Alhambra, the Empire, and the Palace, which though including in their programme an occasional dramatic scene, are chiefly occupied with variety entertainments, there is no temptation to meddle.

CHAPTER XII.

In dealing with the significant growth of new theatres it has been convenient and expedient to treat of successive managements. There are a few managements, however, which are elusive or nomadic. At the head of such must be placed that of Mr. Forbes-Robertson, by general consent the most refined, intellectual and romantic of our younger school of actors. His name has often been encountered since it is met with as a member of that Prince of Wales's company to which the first dawning of a light of renascence has been traced. Alone or in connection with Miss Kate Rorke at the Garrick or Mrs. Patrick Campbell at the Lyceum, and elsewhere, he has frequently come under observation. With so many managements has he been associated that he is somewhat hard to locate. His most interesting experiments were made at the Lyceum under his temporary management of that house. Here he was seen as HAMLET, giving a rendering of that character which disputes supremacy with the HAMLETS of Fechter, Irving, Tree, and other actors, and is in some qualities, notably in limpidity of utterance and faultlessness of execution, first among all. Another performance of extreme interest was that of *Romeo and Juliet*, in which the melodious delivery of Mr. Forbes-Robertson was of wonderful avail, as were the picturesqueness and rhetorical graces of Mrs. Campbell. Among the novelties produced by Mr. Robertson during his tenure of the house the most conspicuous in merit, though scarcely, perhaps, in popularity, was the *Michael and His Lost Angel* of Mr. Henry Arthur Jones. An inspired love poem, such as our drama too seldom supplies, the piece shocked the average public almost as much as it pleased the cultivated. Produced on the 15th January, 1896, it was withdrawn prematurely, just as the more intellectual playgoers were awaking to a knowledge of its quality. As the ascetic priest Mr. Robertson had a class of part in which he has no equal. Miss Marion Terry played the pagan temptress with much seductiveness and feeling. A month later was produced *For the Crown*, a rendering by Mr. John Davidson of M. Coppée's *Pour la Couronne*. In this play Mr. Robertson gave a superb rendering of the loyal son driven to an act of parricide. The female parts were finely rendered by Miss Winifred Emery, Mrs. .Patrick Campbell, and Miss Sarah Brooke; Mr. Ian Robertson, Mr. Mackintosh and Mr. Charles Dalton being seen to advantage. In *Magda*, Mr. Louis N. Parker's translation of *Sudermanna Heimat*, Mrs. Patrick Campbell obtained the crowning success of her career, the full development of which was subsequently seen at the Royalty. Mr. Forbes-Robertson's HEFFTERDINGK was far the best that has been seen in all the renderings of the play that have been given in English, French, Italian, or German. Very satisfactory also was the LEOPOLD SCHWARTZE of Mr. Fernandez.

After the departure of Mr. Forbes-Robertson, the Lyceum, during the absence of Sir Henry Irving, came into the hands of Mr. Martin Harvey, who produced there *The Only Way*, and afterwards into those of Mr. Wilson Barrett, who appeared there in *Man and His Maker*, by himself and Mr. Louis N. Parker, which, in spite of a good interpretation, failed greatly to interest. Revivals of *The Silver King*, *The Sign of the Cross* and *The Manxman* followed. In 1900 Sir Henry Irving and Miss Ellen Terry reappeared, and, under the management of Mr. Comyns Carr, had a season which, devoid of novelty, was brilliantly remunerative.

In 1895 the Royalty—long a home for quaint and sometimes forlorn experiments—awoke, and, with *The Chili Widow* of Messrs. Bourchier and Sutro, showed how much talent as a *comédienne* was possessed by Miss Violet Vanbrugh. Her performance in this adaptation of *Monsieur le Directeur*, by MM. Bisson and Carré, was brilliant. Mr. Arthur Bourchier as SIR REGINALD DELAMERE first established himself in the line of strong comedy in which his recent successes have been made. Other pieces equally light, or even lighter, followed in *The New Baby*, adapted from the German by Mr. Bourchier; and *The Queen's Proctor*, taken by Mr. Herman Merivale from *Divorçons*, in which Miss Violet Vanbrugh, her sister Irene, and Mr. Bourchier were seen. *Monsieur de Paris* revealed Miss Violet Vanbrugh in a gruesome class of parts. In this she obtained a success some were disposed to grudge.

THE STAGE IN THE YEAR 1900: A SOUVENIR.

Miss Louie Freear was then seen in *Oh! Susannah*, and the theatre subsequently witnessed *My Innocent Boy*, by Messrs. G. R. Sims and Merrick, *Young Mr. Yarde* and *A Little Ray of Sunshine*, in which, after an absence from the stage, Mr. Penley reappeared. A special word may be added concerning the Court in its later days, when Mr. Dion Boucicault, an excellent actor who has now transferred his services to Mr. Wyndham, joined the previously existing management of Mr. Arthur Chudleigh. It was on the 20th January, 1898, that the house gave Mr. Pinero's ingenious revival of the days of the crinoline, and his convincing and delightful pictures of theatrical life in his *Trelawny of the Wells*. In this Mr. Dion Boucicault exhibited the best of many character sketches as VICE-CHANCELLOR SIR WILLIAM GOWER, Miss Irene Vanbrugh presented a charming stage type as ROSE TRELAWNY, Mr. Paul Arthur was an admirable TOM WRENCH, and Miss Isabel Bateman, Miss Eva Williams, Mr. G. Du Maurier, Mr. James Erskine and Mr. E. M. Robson did full justice to the eccentric types—chiefly vagabond—Mr. Pinero's genius and fancy had devised. *His Excellency the Governor* was noteworthy as the first important and successful effort of Captain Marshall, an English Marivaux, to whom the stage is indebted for work equally fresh, novel, inspired and delightful, and to whom all are looking forward with sanguine anticipation. *A Royal Family*, which belongs to the latest days of the Court, and had to finish its run elsewhere, is one of the daintiest, archest, and most playful pieces of modern times. It was one of the best acted also. The KING of Mr. Eric Lewis was, perhaps, the most finished impersonations of a highly-finished comedian. In its serene sweetness, dignity, and seriousness it was unequalled. Mr. Dion Boucicault was admirably court-like as the CARDINAL, Mr. Paul Arthur was bright and alert as PRINCE VICTOR CONSTANTINE, Miss Gertrude Elliott was all innocence and charm as the heroine, and Mrs. Calvert, Miss Mabel Hackney, Mr. James Erskine and Mr. Aubrey Fitzgerald did full justice to a fascinating piece.

Though interpreted by a company including Mr. Dion Boucicault, Mr. Paul Arthur, Mr. Gottschalk, Miss Marion Terry, and Miss Irene Vanbrugh, *When a Man's in Love*, by Anthony Hope and Mr. E. Rose, proved too thin for public taste. No more successful was the *Cupboard Love* of Mr. Esmond, though it was well played by Miss May Whitty,

Miss Sibyl Carlisle, Miss Nina Boucicault, Mr. Dion Boucicault, Mr. Herbert Standing, and many clever actors. *A Court Scandal*—an adaptation of *Les Premières Armes de Richelieu*—introduced Miss Miriam Clements and Miss Dorothea Baird, Mr. Seymour Hicks, Mr. Allan Aynesworth, Mr. Brandon Thomas, Mr. Beveridge, and Mr. Pigott; and Mr. Carton's *Wheels Within Wheels* was supported by Miss Compton and Miss Lena Ashwell, Mr. Dion Boucicault, Mr. Eric Lewis, Mr. Thalberg, and Mr. Arthur Bourchier. Both pieces were finely acted. The opening scene of the latter, in which Miss Compton, as MRS. ONSLOW BULMER, "burgles" for a thoroughly honest purpose some bachelor chambers in a fashionable quarter, and has a capital scene with LORD ERIC CHANTRELL, earnestly and brightly played by Mr. Boucicault, was in all senses a treat. On the Court Theatre, however, in these lattermost days had fallen a blight, which even Captain Marshall's delightful play before mentioned could not wholly dispel.

While these lines were being written, at the Globe theatre a novelty has been given in the shape of *Colonel Cromwell*, founded on a romance of Mr. Arthur Paterson entitled *Cromwell's Own*. This stimulating play shows the great Protector in his early life as a wholly worthy, large hearted and sympathetic being. A similar effort had been made with less success in the *Cromwell* of Colonel Alfred Bate Richards, produced at the Queen's on the 21st December, 1879, and intended as an answer to the *Charles I* of Wills. The Globe piece was noticeable for the excellent performance of CROMWELL by Mr. Charles Cartwright, who was part author of the work. Not the first time is this that Mr. Cartwright has given a rugged presentment of the great revolutionary leader. *Colonel Cromwell* has now been withdrawn. It may be added that *Mr. and Mrs. Daventry* and Mr. Frank Harris have brought the Royalty once more into the hands of Mrs. Campbell, who, with Mr. Kerr and Mr. Du Maurier, acts finely in a not very popular or promising piece.

Conducted on the lines adopted which, in a work of this character, are the only lines possible, an account of the progress of the stage seems fragmentary as well as incomplete. The purpose aimed at is realised if the reader is able to see how steady and systematic that progress has been during the last generation; the period of advance cannot be

THE STAGE IN THE YEAR 1900: A SOUVENIR.

extended to half a century. The reconciliation between the stage and the sister arts in the year 1900 is completely re-established. Not an exhibition of the Royal Academy is there on the walls of which are not displayed portraits by our principal painters of our best graced actors, and scarcely an important revival, the decorations, scenery and dresses of which have not been devised by painters of eminence, from a Long to an Alma Tadema. The first musicians of the day not only collaborate with authors, but contribute the incidental music to non-lyrical pieces. The public attracted to a first entertainment at a favourite house is the most brilliant from every standpoint that London can supply. When, moreover, as sometimes happens, a new work that, even of a master, fails wholly to commend itself, the evening of the playgoer has rarely been wasted. Almost to a certainty "the show" is worth seeing if only for the beauty of the decorations, the *ensemble*, and the rhythmic perfection of the acting. Books on the stage multiply; fiction chooses as its heroines stage personages, real or imaginary; and articles on subjects dramatic and histrionic are of constant occurrence in the reviews and magazines, which constitute a large—sometimes one is apt to fear too large—a portion of our reading.

How close is the union between the stage and the highest intellect of the day is best shown in the fact that plays are beginning once more to rank as literature. Few will deny a right to the claim to the title of *Plays, Pleasant and Unpleasant*, by Mr. George Bernard Shaw, which, however much they may on the stage jar on the man deficient in imagination and humour, are wholly delightful in perusal. The collections of printed plays by Mr. Pinero and Mr. Henry Arthur Jones extend over many volumes, and embrace the best works of those authors. Two volumes of Mr. Gilbert's dramas have seen the light, and occasional works by Mr. Haddon Chambers and Mrs. Craigie induce the hope that these writers, Mr. Grundy, Mr. Carton, Captain Marshall, and Mr. Herman Merivale may see their way to print their collected dramas. A selection from the plays of W. G. Wills might well hope for success, and such even has been more than once suggested. It must not be forgotten that the reason for the non-publication of plays—the temptation offered in former days to dishonest managements to dispense with author's fees — no longer exists.

THE STAGE IN THE YEAR 1900: A SOUVENIR.

Of works practically unacted, that is, rarely or never appealing to a general public—such as the fine dramas of Mr. Swinburne—no count is here taken. Tennyson, as the previous record shows, is not unacted, some half-dozen of his works having seen the footlights. Early in the Victorian reign collected dramas were not unknown. Those of Sheridan Knowles, Bulwer Lytton, Sir Henry Taylor, Browning, Talfourd and Douglas Jerrold are easily recalled. Of later productions few were printed. The dramas of Dickens were not collected by the author. We have plays of Ross Neil, one or two of which were acted; a posthumous collection, in no very adequate form, of Robertson's works; two volumes of Westland Marston's works, representing about half his dramatic baggage; a single volume—the publication got no further—of Tom Taylor. Planché published a selection of extravaganzas for a special purpose. The plays of Buckstone, Webster, and innumerable others, principally adaptations, enjoy a repose it would be unwise to disturb, so far as the reading public is concerned. Those of later dramatists—Reade, Watts Phillips, Albery, Boucicault, men of higher dramatic mark—sleep no less soundly, since the acting editions issued for purely professional purposes do not count. Not one of Byron's innumerable plays is accessible in directly literary form. The works of Mr. G. R. Sims, Mr. Cecil Raleigh, Pettitt, and others, scarcely aim at literary fame, though those of Mr. Hamilton Aidé do. Mr. Burnand has printed few of his contributions to the stage. The same may be said of Shirley Brooks, Wilkie Collins, Mr. Robert Buchanan, and many others; while the plays of Mr. J. M. Barrie, Anthony Hope and Bronson Howard—the last an American—are not yet numerous enough to constitute, apart from the novels on which they are sometimes founded, a literary equipment. Mr. Stephen Phillips is approaching the stage by way of the press, and has given to Her Majesty's the greatly conceived drama *Herod*. For the production of *Paolo and Francesca* we still wait.

The dramatic outlook is no less brilliant than that of the stage. The dramatic revival is, however, not to be regarded as coeval with the renascence of the stage. It would scarcely be unjust indeed to describe it in its full development as a growth of the last decade.

It has already been indicated that Robertsonian comedy, bright as this was, did not in itself

THE STAGE IN THE YEAR 1900: A SOUVENIR.

involve a new birth. A happy conjunction of a spirited and intelligent management and a clever and a perceptive dramatist led to the new order of things by which we all benefit. In themselves Robertson's plays were not greatly better than *Money*, *London Assurance*, *Masks and Faces*, *The Game of Speculation*, *A Favourite of Fortune*, or *Cyril's Success*. When those to whom we now look with most pride, gratitude, and hope, first came forward they were not hailed as inaugurating a new state of affairs. *The Silver King* was an admirable melodrama, one of the best that has been seen. It did not entirely blot out memories of *The Colleen Bawn*, *Arrah na Pogue*, *The Two Orphans*, or *The Ticket of Leave Man*. Mr. Pinero's opening effort attracted comparatively little attention.

Mr. Grundy's *The Snowball* gave but slight promise of *Sowing the Wind* and *A Debt of Honour*. Almost alone, Mr. Carton came into the field fully equipped. In his farces, such as *The Magistrate*, *Dandy Dick* and *The Amazons*, Mr Pinero showed himself a delightful writer. We had to wait for *The Second Mrs. Tanqueray*, *The Notorious Mrs. Ebbsmith*, *The Benefit of the Doubt* and *The Gay Lord Quex* before we dared to measure him against the best dramatists of *Outre Manche*. *Michael and His Lost Angel* and *The Masqueraders* showed the height of Mr. Jones's serious power, as *The Case of Rebellious Susan* and *The Liars* of his wit, observation and raillery. Since then has come *Mrs. Dane's Defence*, perhaps the greatest of all. Mrs. Craigie has contributed greatly to our enjoyment, but much more is, we hope, in store. It is useless to continue illustrations of the sort. What is the exact value of our existing drama when measured against France, Germany and Scandinavia cannot be settled until we are able to regard it from a more distant standpoint. That we have a drama delightful to contemplate, and in some cases to read, we know, and we have reasons for a sanguine faith that it has not yet reached its highest development. In dealing with the stage we are on safer ground. We can point unhesitatingly to well nigh a dozen houses at which plays are mounted as well as at any Continental theatre, and to half that number at which the acting is equal to the best that Europe or America can boast. Such is the condition of the stage in 1900. Whether the eminent position in which it stands will be maintained is a part of the future of our mighty country which is beyond our ken, but concerning which there is every right to be hopeful and assured. Some drawbacks, inevitable for the most part, there are. Mr. Toole, who has ministered to innocent mirth and delight longer than any living actor and contributed as largely to the stage of yesterday as to that of to-day, is, we fear, likely to be seen no more in PAUL PRY or CALEB PLUMMER, and to give us no further *Walker, London*. Other fine actors are in retreat or seldom seen. A list of those of high mark of whom we can boast would convert this work into a mere nomenclature.

If it is asked whether any serious menace exists to histrionic art, it seems well to say that there are two sources of danger. Admirably as works the system of actor management—and no lover of art would dream of dispensing with it—it leads at times to such over-elaboration of style in a principal part as destroys the firm balance on which the highest efforts rest. Even more serious is the fact that those in a position to choose their own parts are sacrificing to a wild craving for sympathy the desire to furnish revelations of human character. There are some of our great artists who fail to recognise that a character may be clearer to us because of its infirmities or greater because it is repellent. The attempt to secure sympathy for Iago has not yet been made. There are characters however, from the greatest in Shakespeare down to the latest invention of our existing dramatists, that would be riper, more artistic and more effective, if the attempt at idealisation, and almost as it seems at apotheosis, were abandoned.

Titles in This Series

Criticism: General, Poetic, and Dramatic

1. Alfred Austin. THE POETRY OF THE PERIOD. 1870
2. Robert Buchanan. A LOOK ROUND LITERATURE. 1887
3. John William Cole. THE LIFE AND THEATRICAL TIMES OF CHARLES KEAN, F.S.A. 1859. (In two volumes)
4. E. S. Dallas. POETICS: AN ESSAY ON POETRY. 1852
5. E. S. Dallas. THE GAY SCIENCE. 1866
6. H. Buxton Forman. OUR LIVING POETS: AN ESSAY IN CRITICISM. 1871
7. Walter Hamilton. THE AESTHETIC MOVEMENT IN ENGLAND, third edition, 1882
8. R. H. Horne, editor. A NEW SPIRIT OF THE AGE, second edition. 1844. (In two volumes)
9. Madge Kendall. THE DRAMA. 1884. with DRAMATIC OPINIONS. 1890

10. Joseph A. Knight. A HISTORY OF THE STAGE DURING THE VICTORIAN ERA. 1901

11. Lord William Pitt Lennox. PLAYS, PLAYERS, AND PLAYHOUSES AT HOME AND ABROAD. 1881. (In two volumes)

12. Robert James Mann. TENNYSON'S "MAUD" VINDICATED: AN EXPLANATORY ESSAY. 1856

13. Mowbray Morris. ESSAYS IN THEATRICAL CRITICISM. 1882

14. Henry Neville. THE STAGE: ITS PAST AND PRESENT IN RELATION TO FINE ART. 1875

15. "Q" [Thomas Purnell]. DRAMATISTS OF THE PRESENT DAY. 1871

16. Walter Raleigh. STYLE. 1897

17. William Caldwell Roscoe. POEMS AND ESSAYS (volume two, ESSAYS, only). 1860

18. Clement Scott. THE DRAMA OF YESTERDAY & TODAY. 1899. (In two volumes)

19. James Field Stanfield. AN ESSAY ON THE STUDY AND COMPOSITION OF BIOGRAPHY. 1813

Parody, Satire, Literary Controversy, and Curiosa

20. Edward Bulwer-Lytton. THE NEW TIMON. 1846.

with Algernon Charles Swinburne. SPECIMENS OF
MODERN POETS. THE HEPTALOGIA, OR THE
SEVEN AGAINST SENSE. 1880. with Algernon
Charles Swinburne. "DISGUST: A DRAMATIC
MONOLOGUE." 1898

21. [William E. Aytoun and Theodore Martin.] THE
BOOK OF BALLADS: EDITED BY BON GAULTIER.
1845. with [William E. Aytoun.] FERMILIAN: OR
THE STUDENT OF BADAJOZ: A SPASMODIC
TRAGEDY BY T. PERCY JONES. 1854

22. James Carnegie. JONAS FISHER: A POEM IN
BROWN AND WHITE. 1875. with [A. C.
Swinburne.] THE DEVIL'S DUE: A LETTER TO
THE EDITOR OF "THE EXAMINER." BY THOMAS
MAITLAND. 1875

23. Philip James Bailey. THE AGE; A COLLOQUIAL
SATIRE. 1858

24. [W. C. Bennett.] ANTI-MAUD. 1856. with [Eustace
Clare Grenville Murray.] THE COMING K———
1873. with [W. H. Mallock.] EVERY MAN HIS
OWN POET. 1877

25. [John Burley Waring.] POEMS INSPIRED BY CERTAIN
PICTURES AT THE ART TREASURES EXHIBITION,
MANCHESTER. 1857. with [Anon.] THE LAUGHTER
OF THE MUSES. 1869

26. Robert Buchanan. THE FLESHLY SCHOOL OF POETRY
AND OTHER PHENOMENA OF THE DAY. 1872.

with Algernon Charles Swinburne. UNDER THE MICROSCOPE. 1872

27. J. Rutter. THE NINETEENTH CENTURY, A POEM, IN TWENTY-NINE CANTOS. 1900

Collections of Critical Essays

28. William E. Fredeman, editor. VICTORIAN PREFACES AND INTRODUCTIONS: A FACSIMILE COLLECTION. 1986

29. Ira Bruce Nadel, editor. VICTORIAN FICTION: A COLLECTION OF ESSAYS FROM THE PERIOD. 1986

30. Ira Bruce Nadel, editor. VICTORIAN BIOGRAPHY: A COLLECTION OF ESSAYS FROM THE PERIOD. 1986

31. John F. Stasny, editor. VICTORIAN POETRY: A COLLECTION OF ESSAYS FROM THE PERIOD. 1986

32. William E. Fredeman, editor. THE VICTORIAN POETS: AN ALPHABETICAL COMPILATION OF THE BIO-CRITICAL INTRODUCTIONS TO THE VICTORIAN POETS FROM A. H. MILES'S "THE POETS AND POETRY OF THE NINETEENTH CENTURY." 1986